LIVING
BY THE
WORD

LIVING

BY THE

WORD

Meditations from
The Christian Century

DEBRA BENDIS, ED.
DAVID HEIM, EXEC. ED.

CHALICE
PRESS
ST. LOUIS, MISSOURI

In an effort to make these essays more useful and expansive in their application, certain material has been altered from the essays' original publication in *The Christian Century*. For example, dated material and references have been removed, citations for biblical quotes added, and capitalization style made consistent among the essays.

Bible quotations, unless otherwise noted, are from the *New Revised Standard Version Bible*, copyright 1989, Division of Christian Education of the National Council of the Churches of Christ in the United States of America. Used by permission. All rights reserved.

Scripture quotations marked (NIV) are taken from the HOLY BIBLE, NEW INTERNATIONAL VERSION®. NIV®. Copyright © 1973, 1978, 1984 by International Bible Society. Used by permission of Zondervan Publishing House. All rights reserved.

Bible quotations marked KJV are from the *King James Version Bible*.

Cover art: Digital Stock
Cover and interior design: Elizabeth Wright

Visit Chalice Press on the World Wide Web at
www.chalicepress.com

10 9 8 7 6 5 4 3 2 1   05 06 07 08 09

Library of Congress Cataloging–in–Publication Data

Living by the Word : meditations from the christian century / Debra Bendis, editor.
    p. cm.
  ISBN 10: 0-827221-28-2 (pbk. : alk. paper)
  ISBN 13: 978-0-827221-28-2
  1. Bible—Criticism, interpretation, etc. 2. Devotional calendars. 3. Lectionary preaching. I. Bendis, Debra. II. Christian century (Chicago, Ill. : 1902)
  BS511.3.L585 2005
  251'.6—dc22

                                                           2005007498

Printed in the United States of America

Contents

Contributors

Joanna Adams is a parish pastor at Morningside Presbyterian Church in Atlanta, Georgia.

Mary W. Anderson is pastor of Incarnation Lutheran Church in Columbia, South Carolina.

Stephen Paul Bouman is bishop of the Metropolitan New York Synod of the Evangelical Lutheran Church in America.

Walter Brueggemann is professor emeritus at Columbia Theological Seminary in Decatur, Georgia, and the author of many books and articles.

Fred Craddock is director of the Craddock Center in Cherry Log, Georgia, and the author of many books and articles.

Barbara Crafton is an Episcopal priest, spiritual director, and author of *Finding Time for Serenity* (Morehouse).

Kristen Bargeron Grant is pastor of Cedar United Methodist Church in Ham Lake, Minnesota.

Mary E. Hinkle is associate professor of New Testament at Luther Seminary in St. Paul, Minnesota, and author of *Signs of Belonging: Luther's Marks of the Church and the Christian Life* (Augsburg Fortress).

Paul Keim teaches Bible, religion, and biblical languages at Goshen College in Goshen, Indiana.

William H. Lamar IV is pastor of Greater Saint Paul AME Church in Orlando, Florida.

Bill O'Brien is co-director of BellMitra Associates in Birmingham, Alabama. He served for twenty-one years with the Foreign Mission Board of the Southern Baptist Convention and is author of *Challenges Confronting Baptist Missions* (Baptist History and Heritage Society).

John Ortberg is teaching pastor at Menlo Park Presbyterian Church in Menlo Park, California, and the author of *Everybody's Normal Till You Get to Know Them* (Zondervan).

Barbara Sholis is pastor of First United Methodist Church in Newark, Ohio.

John Stendahl is pastor of Lutheran Church of the Newtons (ELCA) in Newton Centre, Massachusetts.

Paul Stroble teaches at University of Akron in Akron, Ohio, and is the author of *What Do Other Faiths Believe?* (Abingdon Press).

Andrew Warner is a minister at Plymouth United Church of Christ in Milwaukee, Wisconsin.

William H. Willimon is bishop of the Southeastern Jurisdictional Conference of the United Methodist Church.

Patrick Willson is pastor of Williamsburg Presbyterian Church in Williamsburg, Virginia.

Lawrence Wood is pastor of the Fremont United Methodist Church in Fremont, Michigan, and author of *One Hundred Tons of Ice and Other Gospel Stories* (Westminster John Knox Press).

Preface

In 1986, *The Christian Century* published the first "Living by the Word" meditation in its April 5 issue. Kosuke Koyama, former professor at Union Theological Seminary, was the first LBW contributor, followed that same year by Lamin Sanneh and Pheme Perkins.

Century subscribers consistently rate the LBW meditation as a favorite feature, and pastors turn to it as they begin to prepare their sermons. This book begins with the first Sunday of Advent and includes fifty-two meditations, one for each week in Year B of the three-year lectionary cycle (A,B,C).

With the leadership of writers Walter Brueggemann, John Stendahl, Mary B. Anderson, Fred Craddock, and others, the book will also serve as a resource for those who want to enrich a weekly personal devotion time or lead a Bible study.

As always in *Century* endeavors, preparation for this book involved all members of a dedicated staff. Those who worked closely with this project are executive director David Heim, senior editor Debra Bendis, contributing editor Dean Peerman, and intern Martha Summer.

Advent Alchemy

JOHN STENDAHL

Isaiah 64:1–9; Mark 13:24–37; 1 Corinthians 1:3–9

Oh, that you would tear open the heavens and come down,
so that the mountains would quake at your presence!
(Isaiah 64:1)

"Stir up your power O Lord, and come…"

This traditional prayer for the First Sunday in Advent begins with abrupt and urgent entreaty. There is no delay for caressing words of prayerful invocation; rude as a wakening alarm, we call for God to get moving. The collect for the following week will pray for God to stir up our hearts; but now, first, it appears to be the sluggishness of God's heart that is in question. It is God's spirit that first needs stirring to action.

If Advent prepares us for some fresh coming of Christ—at this year's Christmas and/or in that larger future whereby we reimagine our present—then it is a time to acknowledge more deeply the ways that we need God's anointed to come. Lighting our candles, we see ourselves again as dwelling in darkness. Despite all the lights and noise of Christmas commerce, the world is cold and in need. God is not here. Not yet, not enough.

Isaiah prays, "O that you would tear open the heavens and come down, so that the mountains would quake at your presence!" (64:1). If only the heavens would open wide and we would see God's overriding majesty, God's justice and grace revealed to us and to all this sorry world. If only the firmament were rent and goodness poured down into the midst of our lives. If only all that is wrong with this world could be burned away and God's children vindicated and restored.

But the heavens do not open. Not that way. Beneath the firmament, history continues to play out its recurrent ancient tragedies. We ourselves recall seeing the sky's lovely ceiling change to horror and then descend in choking clouds of dust. Even when gazing into a starlit night, we see no heaven revealed on the other side. The stars are not benignly glittering angels. The firmament is not a thin shell but goes on and on into infinite wastes and countless indifferent galaxies. Even in their clarity, the heavens are as opaque as those over Golgotha, where Jesus could no longer find the God to whom he prayed.

Yet even now we are not so different from the prophet of old, nor from Jesus or Paul and all the others who have prayed this way before us. We address the silent heavens and call on the distant Lord whom we cannot see. We urge on the God who seems so slow. Faithfully, like those before us, we enter once again into the drama of yearning and waiting.

Why? What's with this double make-believe that pretends both that we are now waiting for Jesus to be born in Bethlehem and that we really expect the heavens soon to open and reveal the Messiah "'coming in clouds' with great power and glory" (Mk. 13:26b)? Why again these candles and this ritualized longing? After all this time under an unbroken firmament, would not existential resignation and humane ethical resolve be more honest and ennobling?

I suspect that we choose to enact Advent's longing partly because it is preparation for whatever good will come in the holiday ahead, a practical delay of gratification in order that we might be hungry for the feast. Perhaps we can even succeed now in readying ourselves in such a way that what we anticipate will come with the power of something unexpected, a surprise after all.

In addition, it may be that we value the faithful make-believe of Advent simply because hope is sweet and despair is bitter.

Indeed, perhaps we have found in the season's mood of anticipation the first, even the best, gift of Christmas, the one we get to open early.

I tell myself also, each Advent, that there can be something ethically and spiritually edifying about this exercise, this taking care to note the shape of the darkness in which our candles burn. What is the need for which I need Jesus to come and the hurt I want him to heal? Where is the light most needed? If the heavens do open at Christmas, where and with whom will I hear the angels sing? Such inquiries may be helpful, individually and communally, even if nothing stirs above us.

But now I think that there is a mighty human solidarity at stake here as well. I cannot help joining Isaiah and Jesus and Paul and all the rest of them, longing for the heavens to open, for justice to come for the living and the dead, for mercy to make right this damned and beloved world. I will not choose indifference or resignation. I want to be among those who watch and hope, even when the hope feels like despair. It is after all the company in which God chose to be enfleshed, in Jesus, praying to the still unanswering sky.

And perhaps God did then stir in the heavens, unseen above Golgotha. Perhaps those heavens opened for shepherds to hear a song of peace one night, and later on so that the Holy Spirit could attend a baptism at the Jordan River. And perhaps they will at last open for everyone, that every eye may see.

And then sometimes, some blessed times, we have had worked in us such Advent alchemy that our own hearts stir to feel the stirring of God. Not yet so powerful, not yet quite visible, but more, we think, than just imagined. While the sky still appears opaque and silent, seeds quicken in the dark soil. A child stirs in the womb.

On Your Mark

JOHN STENDAHL

Psalm 85:1–2, 8–13; Isaiah 40:1–11; Mark 1:1–8; 2 Peter 3:8–15

The beginning of the good news of Jesus Christ, the Son of God. (Mark 1:1)

Like a starter's pistol, this brief first verse rings out, and Mark's narrative is off and running. We may take the chain of phrases in this verbless sentence simply as a title, the announcement of what follows—the title and then immediately the launch headlong into the story.

As so often in Mark, though, we may pause, or go back to what went by so fast and wonder what it meant. Our first thought may be that here is simply a conventional way to say that at just this point we are beginning the gospel story that follows, that Mark's little book is itself "the good news." But might it actually be, as it seems when read in this lesson, that this first "on your mark" verse heads only this opening portion of the gospel, not the entire gospel? That the witness of John the Baptist is the beginning of the good news, while its fullness is not to be revealed until later?

If that is possible, then perhaps there's more included under this rubric: maybe it's the whole first half of the book that is "the beginning of the good news." The whole Galilean ministry—the attempt of Jesus to make known the kingdom through his teaching—is, after all, just a start. Arguably too, it's a sort of false start, as his message is repeatedly obscured by the cult of his person and power. Thwarted by the misunderstandings of both crowds and disciples, Jesus will resort to a more desperate measure and will make his turn toward the cross. But that comes later.

Then again, maybe it is the whole of Mark's book, or rather what it recounts, that is being described in verse one. It may all be a beginning, the inception of a gospel not so much contained in these pages as it is meant to be alive in the hearers' present and future. Do we perhaps go back to this story, not to look at the past, but to think about how it could or should unfold in our own lives?

As I consider these possibilities, I think about how abrupt the ending of Mark is. The white-clad figure at the tomb tells the women that the risen Jesus has gone ahead to Galilee and that his disciples will see him there, but we're not told what happened next. Did the disciples even get the message? Did they stay in Jerusalem playing church, rather than go back on the dusty campaign trail with Jesus? Did they not understand that he had gone back to renew his mission? He was afoot again in Galilee, the servant of the liberating kingdom. He had gone ahead.

There is ample reason to think that Mark believes the disciples got it wrong once again. But the rough ending of Mark is not really about whether they got the message or not, or about what they did or did not do. It's about those of us who get the message, and who can now continue, if not quite finish, the unfinished gospel. Suddenly the story is in our hands.

And how do we begin to complete it? Remember the words at the tomb: we go back, as it were, to Galilee, back to the place where Jesus began his mission. We go back to the beginning of the gospel, to announcement, hope, and repentance. And maybe this time, knowing what we do now, we will better understand what John the Baptist and Jesus were talking about. Maybe this time we'll repent and believe the good news. We return to reread the story, to start again with fresh ears and a new heart. The title at the beginning of Mark welcomes back those who come again from the empty tomb, seeking Jesus alive and anew.

The signature text and image of Advent in my Swedish childhood was the entry of Jesus into Jerusalem. The crowds, the palms, and the hosannas didn't belong only to Holy Week's darkening narrative; in a lighter, more hopeful key they were also part of the outset of a new church year. We, too, were welcoming Jesus; and he was coming to us again on his borrowed donkey. We were glad to greet him, and God was giving us a new chance to receive him aright this time. The story began again for us, and we rose to it with hope.

Though the Advent use of that entry text has disappeared from our current lectionaries, it still lingers here and there in our hymnody. It is also not far from the themes of the lessons that we read. It connects to the stirring excitement of hope in the prophet's words and in the promises of the psalm. In the second lesson, the apostle describes our waiting for the Lord's coming not as cause for fatigued despair, but as a gracious forbearance, a gift of time to ready ourselves. And at last the voice calls out in the wilderness, preparing the way for the one who comes. A new age begins with cleansing and promise, the gift of a Holy Spirit after the flames.

To be at a beginning is to find that we are not prisoners of the past. John the Baptist announced as much. We and our blessed and foolish land need not be bound to our idolatries or regrets, our greeds or fears. We can begin again.

That's not just a prelude; it is already part of what it anticipates. The "good news of Jesus" was already at work in this expectancy and preparation, the beginning of the beginning. Is it not still so?

Messianic Complex

JOHN STENDAHL

John 1:6–8, 19–28

"I am not the Messiah." (John 1:20b)

John the Baptist baptized Jesus. The synoptic gospels all say so, and the kerygma in Acts connects the beginning of Jesus' ministry with John's baptizing. But although Mark seems to find it quite right that Jesus of Nazareth should have been among those who heeded John's preaching, the three other evangelists appear concerned over the suggestion that Jesus was in some way a disciple of this other preacher.

In Matthew's account, John himself raised the issue and makes clear that he knows who is greater: "I need to be baptized by you" (Mt. 3:14b). Luke offers us another perspective, providing the story in which John is destined from before birth to be the prophet for his younger cousin. Matthew tells of Jesus explaining the baptism was "to fulfill all righteousness" (Mt. 3:15b), and Luke describes the baptism as an occasion of Jesus' solidarity with others and his devotion to God.

The fourth evangelist, however, does not offer an explanation; in fact, he depicts no baptism at all. Instead John the Baptist speaks to the superior authority and divine agency of Jesus. The baptizer does not baptize Jesus but attests to his identity as the Christ and the Lamb of God. "[John] himself was not the light, but he came to testify to the light" (Jn. 1:8). He is explicit both about his own nonmessianic status and about the identity of the one who is anointed.

There may be nothing more to this than the eagerness of the evangelist to brook no rivals to the majestic and powerful Jesus he portrays. Though there are indications in all four of the gospels that John's disciples constitute a sect distinct from the party of Jesus, in the fourth gospel their leader says plainly, "He must increase, but I must decrease" (Jn. 3:30).

Yet perhaps there is more for us here than that, more at stake than a coincidence of rivalry, loyalty, and high christology on the part of the evangelist. Maybe we are to learn something more from John's clear insistence that he is not the Messiah. Maybe we are to learn to say that about ourselves.

"I am not the Messiah."

That negative affirmation may seem obvious, but consider the degree to which faith draws us toward a more positive set of identifications. We are anointed people. We are in Christ, and he lives in us. We are his agents, his hands in the world. We are called to emulate him, to cross the false and imprisoning boundaries of the world with God's transgressively redemptive love. We are to bring good news to the oppressed, to bind up the brokenhearted, to proclaim liberty to the captives and release to the prisoners. As Luther said, we are to be "little Christs," and in no small and timid way. We do have a messianic calling, don't we? We are needed and called to do what Jesus would be doing.

All of that is true and worthy to be recalled. But in John the Baptist's denial is the opposite point, and it too speaks needed truth. Who am I? Who are you? *Not* the Messiah.

Messianic ambitions for ourselves and messianic expectations of others are not just the quaint delusions of people certified as mentally ill. They are found in us and around us as we seek too much from others or wish to be too much to them. In a song that is at once poignant and cruel, Bob Dylan wrote one version of John's denial: "\It ain't me, babe… / It ain't me you're looking for."

The messianic impulse, the assumed role of rescuer of the other, can be an egoism that diminishes and destroys. And the disempowering reciprocal expectation that this special person will be one's savior is not limited to the private and personal spheres of life. These are issues in international relations, in the interplay of social movements and classes, and in political appeals. We have seen dangerous faith placed in false and flawed messiahs. Many of us pray very hard over the particular messianic arrogance that often drives our own nation and its policies.

In this context, it is salutary for us to remember John's pointing away from himself and to Jesus. We are not, any nor all of us, the Messiah. That position has already been filled. To let Jesus be our Christ, our anointed savior and rescuer, may still entail seeking to be engaged in his saving work and mission—of course it does. But it also commands us to humility, a letting go of our seducing desires either to rescue or to be rescued by others. We already have a Messiah, and he ain't us.

In John's gospel, this needed humility is worked by focusing on the person of the beloved Jesus, the revelation that he is the Truth and the Way and the Life. He is the light to which both John the Baptist and John the evangelist were sent to testify.

In the synoptics, however, and especially in Mark, focusing on Jesus reveals something quite curious: it is a quality of the Messiah to do something very like what John the Baptist does here. Jesus points away from himself and seeks to deflect the messianic expectations put upon him. Trying to evade his superstar status and the attributions of glory, he points instead to what is near and soon and already stirring in the lives of those to whom he speaks.

Mary Says Yes

JOHN STENDAHL

Luke 1:26–38, 47–55

At Christmas even the most Protestant among us can be drawn to the contemplation of Mary. It seems right to recall her humble courage, her receiving and carrying and giving birth, and her joy as she sang of the saving work of God. The old *King James Version* puts part of Mary's doxology this way: "He hath scattered the proud in the imagination of their hearts" (Lk. 1:51b). Those words seem especially apt to me, for it is indeed by our imagining, by what our hearts picture in fear or desire, that we humans are pushed and pulled in our many directions.

Yet if imagination is such a medium for our destruction, could it not also serve to gather and bless us? Instead of imagining fantasies and terrors, may we not imagine ourselves alongside Mary, seeing history's hard cruelty give way to hope and gracious surprise? We sing her song of praise and envision the vindication of the poor. We picture her child newborn as if we ourselves held him in our arms, as if God thus came to us as well. By "making believe," we may in fact come to believe. Yet more, what we imagine may take on flesh and truth before our eyes.

I think that we practice this imagination of the heart, by the gift and command of God, in our worship. We make believe that love rules already, that the lowly are lifted up, death conquered, sin cleansed away, peace triumphant, and Christ touched and seen and tasted. On the verge of Christmas, we imagine and sing with Mary in this way.

Yet grateful as I am for her example and companionship in this, there are a couple of things about Mary, or about our churchly imagination of her, that trouble me. The first might be termed an ethical worry. It is that we who are privileged play at a nativity-scene peasanthood and join in the song of Mary without placing our real lives in its context. The Magnificat may move us with its dream of redistributive justice, but do we make imaginative solidarity with Mary only to domesticate her to our decidedly inexpensive fantasies of peace on earth? Are we drawn to consider what this will cost us and to begin paying that price?

I pray that we who have much of the world's goods and power will hear Mary's words about the proud and rich as warnings and salutary threats to ourselves. If we are able to sing those words lustily, let it be because we are seduced by the grandeur and grace of the salvation she describes, but let it also join us to those who yearn for a turning of the socio-economic tables. I fear that we will instead use her as a talisman, a manger set figure, in order to feel as if we're already on the right side of the revolution she sings about. She ought to be more humanly real and powerful than that.

I also worry that Mary will be easily domesticated to my ethical evasions because she is often pictured as meekly compliant. And there begins my second, more theological, Marian discomfort, having to do with the themes of power and consent in this story of our salvation. Part of this is Luke's vision. His gospel is known for its attention to women, but they are portrayed in accord with his strong emphasis on piety and filial obedience. The banter and hard questioning we hear from women in the other gospels is hardly prominent, if even present, in Luke's imagining. His Mary can seem a paragon of compliance.

Perhaps we are intended to see the contrast between Mary's assent—"Let it be with me according to your word" (Lk. 1:38b)—and the primordial disobedience of Eve. The implication is that womanhood, or the soul of all our humanity, will be redeemed not in self-assertion but in abnegation and subordination. We may resist that ideological paradigm and its implications, but it seems near at hand in the account of Gabriel's visit to Nazareth.

Indeed, the angelic annunciation is not worded as a proposal but as an exercise of irresistible power: "The Holy Spirit will come upon you, and the power of the Most High will overshadow you" (Lk. 1:35a). Our piety may protect us from seeing an analogy here with the rape of Io, mighty Zeus covering a woman in the shape of a dark cloud, but even without such blasphemous association the suggestion of patriarchal violence lurks in the story's shadows.

And yet I think we can hear something else in the assent of Mary. To me it seems as if her yes has transfigured the story, for now it hinges on her word, her participation and presence in the drama. That's the kind of story the Bible repeatedly tells. The suggested pattern is no longer so much of divine imposition as one in which Gabriel and God and all the heavens stand in breathless suspense. All history, the salvation of the world, now seems to hang on this one young woman's answer.

Like the assent of Job to God's cosmic majesty in Archibald MacLeish's *J.B.*, gentling God the way one would gentle "a bulging, bugling bull,"Mary's consent subtly recasts the story of power. It is as if the grand God of Israel has become for us—is willing to be for us—like Myles Standish, dispatching Gabriel as a substitute suitor to plead his case. The case may be pressed with claims of power and promises of blessing, but still the ancient one trembles and waits for an answer.

Imagine that. Imagine that he's waiting for us too.

Holding Promise

JOHN STENDAHL

Luke 2:22–40

Picture the old man with the baby in his arms. He stands chuckling with giddy joy, or perhaps he gazes with streaming tears on his cheeks, or is lost in transfixed wonder; in whatever way, he is so very happy. Then he says that this is enough now, he is ready to die. He has seen salvation and he can depart in peace.

But what has he seen, really? It's just a little child in his arms, a powerless, speechless newcomer to the world. Whatever salvation this baby might work is still only a promise and a hope; whatever teaching he might offer will remain hidden for many years. Nothing has happened yet. Herod still sits on his throne and Caesar governs from afar. The world looks as it did before.

But Simeon stands there in grateful wonder. It is the future he holds in his hands. He has seen and touched it. He is satisfied. It is, as he said, enough. And then Anna, also old and approaching the end of her days, adds her own joy and praise to the moment. She'll be telling everybody about this baby whom she saw for just a few minutes.

By the time a mature Jesus comes onto the stage of history, Simeon and Anna will be long dead. So will most of those shepherds who came to see the child in the manger, and possibly Joseph, who watched over him, and some or all of the magi who feature in the other nativity story. Thirty years or more will pass before the gospel story recommences in the ministry of Jesus. In the meantime they who saw the baby, knelt at the stable, or laid their tributes before him would not know what became of him. They would know only what they had heard and seen back then.

Though some might take this aspect of the stories as no more than an accidental effect of nativity prologues for the gospels, it seems to me to offer us both connection and encouragement. We too are people who have seen something but not its full unfolding. Paradoxically, Simeon and Anna do not so much belong to the gospel's prehistory as they are paradigmatic for our own experience of that gospel.

What we have, in a sense, is hardly more than they had. We have the scriptures that school us in hope and attentiveness. We have stories and covenants and signs. We have moments, or the memory of moments, when the tender compassion of our God has come close enough to see and feel. We have something like the shepherds would have had, recalling all their lives a night of mysterious glory, or like what the magi brought back to their homelands, a vision of a different kind of king and kingdom. Their eyes had seen the glory of Israel, the light for the nations.

We have that as well, though for us the world has resumed its accustomed form and, in the light of day, seems largely unsaved and unchanged.

We have also the children now briefly entrusted to our arms for blessing and who will, we hope, live on after us. We pray that their lives will be grand with wisdom and courage and that they will make the world better. As we get older, life becomes increasingly about them and less and less about us. When I hold a child in my arms, as Simeon cradled Jesus in his, my life seems literally recentered: not in myself but just in front of me there. It is around this present future, this vulnerable and miraculous little one, that my universe bends.

You may argue that we have much more than Simeon and the other prologue-dwellers did because we have the rest of the gospel story. We know what happened to the baby and understand more fully the pattern of his life. We know his teaching and the pattern of his passion and vindication. But note that Luke describes Simeon as fairly clued in on that score as well, telling Mary of the conflict and the sorrow that lay ahead. We have no significant advantage even there.

What we have is in these ways hardly more than what Simeon had. But what that is, is wonderful indeed. The canticle he prays has become for much of the church a song to follow the communion meal. We have now seen and tasted the promised future. We have held the Christ child. Taking bread and wine to our lips, we have kissed him and with words and songs we have caressed his presence. We may not get all the way to his future ourselves, not in this life—but we've seen it, and that's enough, we say. We can go in peace now.

But is it really enough? Are we not both ethically and spiritually called to dissatisfaction with such partiality? Should there not be more, and should not the blessing be made something present rather than just a memory of the past or a hope of heaven? Having tasted the kingdom's presence, we hunger and thirst the more for it. Having seen it, we strive to bring it home. Frustrated and yearning, we call for God no longer to tarry, to fulfill the promise, to give us today the bread of tomorrow.

That's all true, but with that struggle and longing we may be the more grateful for the spirit of Simeon and for those times we find ourselves with him. His song has become a sort of Christian "Dayenu," that great Passover song that proclaims each little part of the salvation as sufficient and great enough. We may want more than this manna, but still our hearts lift in thanksgiving.

We have seen. It's enough for now.

Off by Nine Miles

WALTER BRUEGGEMANN

Isaiah 60:1–7; Matthew 2:1–12

Matthew is not the first one to imagine some rich wise guys from the East coming to Jerusalem. His story line and plot come from Isaiah 60, a poem recited to Jews in Jerusalem about 580 B.C.E. These Jews had been in exile in Iraq for a couple of generations and had come back to the bombed-out city of Jerusalem. They were in despair. Who wants to live in a city where the towers are torn down and the economy has failed, and nobody knows what to do about it?

In the middle of the mess, an amazing poet invites his depressed, discouraged contemporaries to look up, to hope and to expect everything to change. "Arise, shine; for your light has come" (Isa. 60:1a). The poet anticipates that Jerusalem will become a beehive of productivity and prosperity, a new center of international trade. "Nations shall come to your light, / and kings to the brightness of your dawn" (Isa. 60:3). Caravans loaded with trade goods will come from Asia and bring prosperity. This is cause for celebration. God has promised to make the city work effectively in peace, and a promise from God is very sure.

Like Matthew, the wise men know about Isaiah 60. They know they are to go to Jerusalem and to take rare treasures, gold and frankincense and myrrh. Most important, they know that they will find the new king of all peace and prosperity. But when Herod (the current king in Jerusalem) hears of these plans, he is frightened. A new king is a threat to the old king and the old order.

Then a strange thing happens. In his panic, Herod arranges a consultation with the leading Old Testament scholars, and says to them, "Tell me about Isaiah 60. What is all this business about camels and gold and frankincense and myrrh?" The scholars tell him: You have the wrong text. And the wise men outside your window are using the wrong text. Isaiah 60 will mislead you because it suggests that Jerusalem will prosper and have great urban wealth and be restored as the center of the global economy. In that scenario, the urban elites can recover their former power and prestige and nothing will really change.

Herod does not like that verdict and asks, defiantly, "Well, do you have a better text?" The scholars are afraid of the angry king, but tell him, with much trepidation, that the right text is Micah 5:2–4:

But you, O Bethlehem of Ephrathah…
from you shall come forth for me
one who is to rule in Israel,
whose origin is from of old…

This is the voice of a peasant hope for the future, a voice that is not impressed with high towers and great arenas, banks and urban achievements. It anticipates a different future, as yet unaccomplished, that will organize the peasant land in resistance to imperial threat. Micah anticipates a leader who will bring well-being to his people, not by great political ambition, but by attentiveness to the folks on the ground.

Herod tells the Eastern intellectuals the truth, and the rest is history. They head for Bethlehem, a rural place, dusty, unnoticed, and unpretentious. It is, however, the proper milieu for the birth of the One who will offer an alternative to the arrogant learning of intellectuals and the arrogant power of urban rulers.

The narrative of Epiphany is the story of these two human communities: Jerusalem, with its great pretensions, and Bethlehem, with its modest promises. We can choose a "return to normalcy" in a triumphalist mode, a life of self-sufficiency that contains within it its own seeds of destruction. Or we can choose an alternative that comes in innocence and a hope that confounds our usual pretensions. We can receive life given in vulnerability. It is amazing—the true accent of epiphany—that the wise men do not resist this alternative but go on to the village. Rather than hesitate or resist, they reorganize their wealth and learning, and reorient themselves and their lives around a baby with no credentials.

Bethlehem is nine miles south of Jerusalem. The wise men had a long intellectual history of erudition and a long-term practice of mastery. But they had missed their goal by nine miles. It is mind-boggling to think how the story might have gone had Herod's interpreters not remembered Micah 2.

Our task is to let the vulnerability of Micah 2 disrupt the self-congratulation of Isaiah 60. Most of us are looking in the wrong place. We are off by nine miles. We are now invited to travel those hard, demanding miles away from self-sufficiency. Epiphany is a good time to take the journey as we consider what the rest of the world thinks of our excessive national pretension. The way beyond is not about security and prosperity but about vulnerability, neighborliness, generosity, a modest future with spears turned into pruning hooks and swords into plowshares.

The wise men, and the eager nations ready for an alternative, made the trip. It would be ironic if the "outsiders" among us made that move and we who are God's own people resisted. Imagine a nine-mile trip…and a very different way home.

A Watery Solution

Barbara Sholis

Genesis 1:1–5; Mark 1:4–11

And just as he was coming up out of the water, he saw the heavens torn apart and the Spirit descending like a dove on him. And a voice came from heaven, "You are my Son, the Beloved; with you I am well pleased." (Mark 1:10–11)

The covenant for holy baptism, found in the *United Methodist Book of Worship,* tells the biblical story of water. "Eternal Father," the story begins, "when nothing existed but chaos, you swept across the dark waters and brought forth light. In the days of Noah you saved those on the ark through water. After the flood, you set in the clouds a rainbow. When you saw your people as slaves in Egypt, you led them to freedom through the sea. Their children you brought through the Jordan to the land which you promised. In the fullness of time you sent Jesus, nurtured in the water of a womb." From that first instant of creation, water has played midwife to God's creation story.

The midwives of my own baptism were the church ladies of a Southern Baptist congregation. I was baptized on a warm April night in Kentucky. Candlelight in the rotunda reflected the sacredness of the moment as I waded into the warm water of the baptismal pool and let the pastor's firm grasp cradle me. I held my nose and was submerged in the water of new birth while he invoked the Father, Son, and Holy Ghost. When I came up out of the water, the bright light startled me. I saw my proud family. Then the church midwives, smelling of hand lotion and dressed in flowered shirtwaist dresses and strings of pearls, wrapped me in a warm towel and handed me my baptismal certificate. I tried to take it all in. Something had happened, but I wasn't quite sure what it was. As Heather Murray Elkins says, I had been sealed with the imago Christi, a permanent tattoo. Yet nothing was visible. What did this baptism mean for my life now?

I think of Robert Duvall in the movie *Tender Mercies*. Duvall plays Mac, a down-on-his-luck country songwriter who battles the bottle. He fights back with the help of a young widow who offers him room and board at her roadside Texas motel in exchange for handyman help. Grace finds a toehold in Mac's life, and eventually both Mac and the widow's young boy, Sonny, make the decision to be baptized. Driving home after the baptism, Sonny says to Mac: "Well, we done it Mac, we was baptized." Peering into the truck's rearview mirror, Sonny studies himself for a moment. "Everybody said I'd feel like a changed person. Do you feel like a changed person?" "Not yet," replies Mac. "You don't look any different, Mac." "Do you think I look any different?" "Not yet," answers Mac. Like Sonny, we don't always see ourselves as changed people. There are times when we can perceive who and where we are only by looking into the rearview mirror and observing the people, places, and events that have passed us by.

Even those in the center of Mark's gospel, Jesus' own disciples, are often looking into the rearview mirror, trying to figure out what just happened. Ironically, those on the periphery—the woman with the hemorrhage, the man possessed by the legion of demons, Jarius—know exactly who this Christ is. By the end of this first chapter, so do we. "And just as he was coming up out of the water," Mark writes, "he saw the heavens torn apart and the Spirit descending like a dove on him. And a voice came from heaven, 'You are my Son, the Beloved; with you I am well pleased.'"

Scholar Donald Juel writes that it is at this moment that the barrier between heaven and earth is removed. No longer is God a distant, impervious God sitting on a throne in the distant heavens. God now comes to dwell among us. God is with us; and as Juel says, God "is on the loose in our realm," swooping into our world like a dove. Jesus, anticipated by John the Baptist as "the one who is coming," comes down from the hills of Nazareth to the baptismal waters of the Jordan River; and the dove descends toward Jesus, signifying that this is the one who embodies God's prophesy. Humanity's relationship with God is transformed. The same creative force that moved across the formless void at creation now tears open the heavens and descends like a dove, making incarnate this new covenant.

Inevitably, life has a way of wringing us out, and we forget that God dwells in and among us. We forget our "beloved" identity. Laurence Hull Stookey labels our forgetfulness "spiritual amnesia" but adds that baptism is what counters our amnesia. The touch of water upon our lives helps us recall our place in the biblical story, and reminds us that God's creative force is still birthing us, claiming us, renewing us.

Many nights have come and gone since I passed through the waters of baptism that warm April night. At times life's circumstances or my own regrettable choices have dimmed my remembrance of God's promise for my life. At first glance into the rearview mirror, I still see only a rebellious creature. But if I really gaze into the mirror, I also see a water mark, a permanent tattoo, that imago Christi, reminding me of my baptism and the One who calls me to be the beloved daughter with whom God is well pleased.

Call Me

PAUL KEIM

1 Samuel 3:1–10; Psalm 139:1–6, 13–18; John 1:43–51

> *Your eyes beheld my unformed substance.*
> *In your book were written*
> *all the days that were formed for me,*
> *when none of them as yet existed. (Psalm 139:16)*

I don't carry a beeper or a cell phone. After all, the services of professional biblical scholars rarely require that level of immediate access. No emergency calls to interpret an obscure passage. No rushing to the scene of a textual corruption. Yet it could happen. We are rapidly becoming a society "on call." "Call me," our equipment says. "I'm here." So why not Semitic philologists on call? "Hello? Yes, I see. Let me just grab my triconsonantal root extractor, and I'll be right there!"

In the midst of all this calling, how do we recognize God's voice calling us? Long ago, even before the rotary phone, the boy Samuel faced a similar dilemma. Calls from Yahweh were rare. But as a child pledged to service in the temple of Yahweh at Shiloh, Samuel was called by name at all times of day and night.

On one particular night, the boy hears his name called, and responds, "Hello? Yes? Here I am. What do you want?"

If you're Eli, you're not sleeping that well when the boy comes trotting in to disturb you with his nonsense. Now even the pretense of slumber is gone; it's just you and your premonitions, a vague sense of doom hanging over you, and the Lord silent as only the Lord can be silent. Prophets wouldn't know a vision anymore if it bit them in the behind. So what's eating the kid? indigestion? fleas? those worthless, carousing sons of yours? No, that boy is sharp. Maybe this is one of those rare cases of a divine call. If it happens again, you'd better instruct the boy how to respond. Just in case.

If you're Samuel, you think it must be the old man. But the temple lamp hasn't even burned out yet, too early for him to be calling for the vessel. He says he didn't call? What? You suspect his eyesight isn't the only thing fading fast. Then there it is again. And again he denies calling you.

This episode is framed by two oracles: the priestly house of Eli is about to fall because of corruption, and a new priest, this Samuel, will be consecrated in his place. The house of this new priest will eventually also fail the test of faithful succession. But for now Eli provides the guidance Samuel needs to hear the call. This role of mentor, facilitator, and arbiter of God's call is crucial to the story. He encourages and instructs Samuel to listen and tells him what to say, then forces the reluctant youth to articulate the message even though it presages his own doom.

In our day, the word of the Lord is cheap, visions are widespread, and telemarketers call us by name. How do we distinguish God's call? Who will play Eli for us and reorient our attention so that we become able receptors of the divine vocation? Can we discern unrecognized, unarticulated vocations in the tossings and turnings and confusions of the young? Are we providing them with the disciplines of heart and mind to listen and to act? Consider Samantha, who hears a call. Imagine Eli saying, "No, it can't be a call to pastoral ministry. You must be mistaken. Go back, teach, write, nurture. That's your vocation."

The calling of Nathanael is less direct—mediated by Philip in the form of an enthusiastic invitation to follow the One from Nazareth. But Nathanael knows Nazareth. Nazareth is *Nowhere*. Nazareth is *Nothing*. A Nazarean is a *Nobody*. A Nichtsnutz.

When I was a kid, the label "made in Japan" signified a cheap trinket that cost little and was worth even less. It was a common term of derision applicable to any product shoddily made or easily broken. But by the time I was in college, the reputation of Japanese technology and workmanship was being transformed. Now, "made in Japan" signifies quality and reliability in a whole range of products.

Nathanael's assumptions about the impossibility of a divine call from Nazareth had to undergo similar transformation. This time Philip is the catalyst who overcomes Nathanael's categoric dismissal: Come and see! *Venit. Vidit. Variatus est.* Nathanael came, saw, and was changed in an encounter made possible by a Philipian invitation and a Philipian coax.

A sense of calling represents a step toward greater self-awareness. To become aware of a call is to be aware of oneself in a new way, as the psalmist was aware: You know me, O Lord. You've done the research. You've read my file. Through the call I know myself as someone known; my life as something comprehended from beginning to end; my days as already written in that book "when none of them as yet existed." This is no recipe for fatalistic determinism, but rather a profound metaphor providing a way out of the modern dilemma. In the place of an alienated self at the center of an arbitrary, amoral universe, or a postmodern ghost trying to conjure up its name through myriad manipulations, we choose to live as those known and called by name.

Of course, every call to something may also be a call away from something. The call that led me to graduate studies coincided with an awareness that teaching high school was not my vocation. This message was brought home in an episode that was tanta-mount to an out-of-the-body experience. At the end of another exasperating day I found myself looking down from a vantage point somewhere near the ceiling of my small classroom at a guy wearing my clothes who was vigorously admonishing a hapless student sitting near the back of the Bible class. Watching the event unfold from this neutral perspective worked as an epiphany. The writing on the wall was ominous but also strangely comforting: *Mene. Mene. Tekel.* I was off to seminary.

Mutant Ministry

PAUL KEIM

Jonah 3:1–5; Psalm 62:5–12; 1 Corinthians 7:29–31

> *And the people of Nineveh believed God; they proclaimed a*
> *fast, and everyone, great and small, put on sackcloth.*
> *(Jonah 3:5)*

Many erstwhile human encounters with the divine word are fraught with irony. The Bible is full of examples: Balaam's talking ass; the promise of a patriarchal heir so long overdue that the child is named for the ensuing hilarity; the virtuous foreign woman deemed to be worth seven times the family-redeeming child she bears for her mother-in-law; the messianic Savior born in a hovel and killed like a common criminal.

The mutant ministry of the prophet Jonah is another case in point. So familiar are the details of this entertaining story that a brief summary will suffice to set the scene. The Prophet of the Lord (PL) is commissioned to warn the Most Evil Empire (MEE) of its impending destruction. The PL flees by boat in the opposite direction. An act of God on the high seas threatens to destroy the ship and all aboard. Phoenician sailors, more deeply religious than the PL, determine who is to blame for the predicament and what to do about it. Despite their reluctance to risk the loss of life (wink, wink), the Phoenician sailors toss the PL into the sea. A large marine creature promptly swallows the PL. From the belly of the whalelike fish, the PL delivers himself of a prayer so lousy with pious platitudes that the poor sea creature pukes him up onto dry land.

Our text begins with a prophetic recall and recommissioning. This time it's off to the MEE. In the midst of the great city the recalcitrant PL unleashes a five-word oracle whose brevity is matched only by its banality: Forty days…and you're toast! (Jonah 3:4, paraphrased). And yet in this exquisite farce, the response far exceeds that of modern, urban, evangelistic crusades among the well-churched. The evil people of the MEE believe in God and exhibit a repentance so robust that a fast is proclaimed and all are clothed in sackcloth, from king to cattle.

God's response is predictable. The whole judgment thing is called off. But the PL is not pleased. His hatred of Nineveh is greater than God's mercy. This is exactly why he had fled in the first place. He wanted no part in the deliverance of the MEE. By the end of the story the PL may or may not have accepted the counterintuitive morality so prevalent throughout the Bible: Samaritans can be good neighbors; stutterers can be lawgivers; theophanies are likely to be encountered in the still, small voice; and not even Nineveh is beyond God's compassion.

This unique prophetic book provokes one to imagine that someone was goofin' with the gullible. Here is prophetic minimalism gone amok. Jonah is portrayed as the moral equivalent of a cliché, the misanthrope in a sandwich board that says "The End Is Near." But perhaps the key lies not in the content of the oracle but in the context of its delivery. The inherent warning of Jonah's oracle is muted in the text. Instead what emerges is a great city paradigmatically pregnant with evil, and rushing toward ruin—or redemption.

A parallel dynamic can be seen in the temporal framework of Paul's ethic. The Corinthians want answers to their questions. How should they live? Paul gives some instructions intended to carry apostolic freight. He wants them to "stay as they are," with some concessions. His rationale is the "impending crisis." The culmination of an appointed time (*kairos*) is just around the corner. From now on they are to live "as if" and "as if not," since the present form of the world is passing away. It's nothing less than the end of the world as they know it. For Paul, the impending wrap-up of history is so vivid that it infuses all current questions, problems, dilemmas, and challenges. If indeed the present form of the world is passing, he seems to reason, why waste energy on lesser orders of concern, such as slavery and sex? These eschatological convictions have shaped Paul's mission and his priorities.

When we hear this kind of imagery bandied about today we think of doomsday cults, survivalist bunkers, and other forms of spiritual excess. But could it not also be used to describe our experience of the modern world? A world seemingly being remade with every passing day. A world less predictable, less comprehensible, in a constant state of flux. In nature and culture, present forms are becoming extinct. Our culture lurches, groaning, toward ruin—or redemption. Something new is coming that we can't quite see. But we feel ourselves at a threshold…

Paul's perspective suggests that we, like the Corinthians, learn to live as if the preoccupations of the present world were not preeminent. To live as if the inevitability and reality of the new order were already transforming the way we live. It is something short of a realized eschatology, perhaps. Nonetheless, even before it arrives, the new thing is forming us, rearranging our priorities.

From the psalmist's perspective, more metaphysical than temporal, priorities are also realigned by God's omnipotence. Low estate and high estate, considerations so crucial in earthly terms, are lighter than a breath in the cosmic balance. To confess that power and loving-kindness belong to God is to relieve ourselves of a significant existential burden, and also to accept an ethical mandate. For the Bible insists that we bear responsibility for the way we live. This principle appears over and over again in scripture, from the law to the prophets to the Lord's Prayer. Forgive us our debts, as we forgive our debtors. Bounded by God's justice and God's mercy, there is this moral universe in which we move and breath and have our being.

Called to Order

PAUL KEIM

Deuteronomy 18:15–20; Psalm 111; 1 Corinthians 8:1–13

> *The LORD your God will raise up for you a prophet like me*
> *from among your own people; you shall heed such a prophet.*
> *(Deuteronomy 18:15)*

Holy Moses! The first surprise in this passage from Deuteronomy is that the biblical lawgiver par excellence is also the prototypical prophet. In twenty-first–century America, prophets are not so easily disguised as congressmen and senators. What does Washington have to do with Waco? Law, or the codification, enforcement, and interpretation of community mores, does not usually appear in the same sentence as prophecy, the impassioned oraculation of the divine word. We tend to think of these two matrices of authority as in tension or opposition to one another. *Vox populi* on the one hand; *Vox dei* on the other.

But in the context of Deuteronomy, the biblical passage reflects a revolutionary program of centralized and perhaps domesticated religious authority. All law and prophecy were to be associated with the offices of prophet, priest, and king in Jerusalem. Previously acceptable forms of divination and worship were to be focused on "the place where the LORD your God Yahweh shall choose to cause his name to dwell" (Deut. 12:11, KJV). The magical practices of the original inhabitants of the land were rejected not only as "Canaanite," but also as illicit soothsaying and divining happening outside the confines of formally sanctioned religion. In place of these practices, a prophet like Moses would be raised up to mediate God's word. Within the order of the ethos of Torah— also conceived of as divine word—the prophet would give voice to the moral imperative.

Within the delimitations of Torah there is accountability for both people and prophet. If the prophet faithfully delivers God's spoken word to the people, the people are held responsible to follow its dictates. If, however, the prophet presumptuously speaks a word that God did not speak, the prophet is held accountable.

How do listeners know when the word spoken by the prophet in the name of Yahweh is not commanded by Yahweh? The answer: if the word turns out not to be true or the prediction does not come to pass, then it is evident that it was not a true word of Yahweh, but only prophetic hauteur. The people are not to be cowed by such a soothsayer.

It's been said that the lessons of history are never clear; and when they are, they're usually wrong. Whereas the principle set forth in Deuteronomy may provide some means of measuring the accuracy of the predictions of an astrologer like Jeane Dixon or the lucrative prognostications of a dispensationalist like Hal Lindsey, it is less well suited to discerning the reliability of a call to moral judgment and decisive action. We may still be left with the dilemma of how to tell the true word from the false.

We are not left, however, without resources for this task. Does the call to moral discernment accord with the ethos of Torah? Scripture can provide tools that help us detect the true texture of history and the interwoven inclinations of God's saving acts. This is something less than blessed assurance. But it does provide an ordered framework within which we can exercise our capacity for moral judgment.

Of course, well-known dangers are associated with all sanctioned and centralized moral orders. They may become self-legitimizing thickets of power that co-opt the moral prerogative of people and prophet and are no longer open to the living word. But biblical tradition refuses to allow God's law to become identified with the king's law. Israelite prophecy could embrace the contemplative order of Mosaic law to call the nation toward faithfulness. The inherent tensions between law and prophecy were not resolved, but there was access to the divine word in an ordered cosmos where people could live as free moral agents.

In the poetic structure of the psalm of praise a different kind of order lives. The acrostic poem adheres to a specific structure in which each line begins with the subsequent letter of the alphabet. Within the discipline of this poetic convention, virtually impossible to reflect in translation, the theme of praise for God's mighty acts unfolds. The construct compels the poet to paint her picture in a given frame, while the conventions of frame and phraseology help focus the attention of the reciter and facilitate memory as well as meditation. Again, freedom within order.

In Paul's teaching concerning the issue of food offered to idols, he refers to a certain kind of theological order: there is *one* God. The gods that the idols are supposed to represent do not exist. Therefore it is lawful to eat food offered to such idols.

But then he weighs this "order of knowledge" against another order—that of Christian love. In this dichotomy, it is acceptable to eat the food offered to idols unless this exercise of one's freedom threatens the conscience of another believer. Then it is sin. It is better to choose self-restraint than to violate the principle of Christian love.

The order of the law and the prophets is a theological one that rests on a foundation of faith. It is not ultimately upheld by any orthodoxy or orthopraxy, by shrill pieties or by militant fundamentalisms. Nor is it undermined by secular science, by modern alienation, or by failed ideologies. Nor can the ache of its absence be felicitously replaced by the comforts of consumerism, or by a pax Americana. It is God's faithfulness, rather than ours, that grounds our being. Within the ordered constraints of our physicality and mortality, we are free to respond to that faithfulness with every capacity that our miraculously evolved consciousness allows. Free to pit lives of healing and hope against a world of chaos and conflict. Free to live with integrity and die with dignity.

No Comparison

PAUL KEIM

Psalm 147:1–11; Isaiah 40:21–31

To whom then will you compare me,
*   or who is my equal? says the Holy One. (Isaiah 40:25)*

Isaiah faced a challenge. How was he to awaken an exiled community from the lethargy of despair? The people's confidence had been shattered. Their entire worldview was drained of its mimetic properties. Former glories lay in ruins. Now the people lived in the land of the dreaded enemy, reciting litanies of lamentation while ghouls goaded them on with, "Sing us some of those songs of Zion, miserable losers! Celebrate the memory of what no longer exists." Psalm 137 records the agony of exile and culminates in a cathartic curse.

But in the taunt lurks a solution, a strategy used by untold generations of the conquered: Take the lemon of the oppressor and make lemonade. Using a series of rhetorical questions, the prophet pushes aside the numbness that is our common defense against pain. Who created this? He asks. Who sustains that? Don't you know? Haven't you heard? Why do you keep on chanting that your way is hidden from Yahweh, that your plight is disregarded by God? Don't you know? ("Of course you know!") Haven't you heard? ("Of course you have!")

Remember the temple psalms of praise, Isaiah urges. You've heard of God's might because you've sung about it! The descriptions of God's mighty acts of creation in the oracle are retrieved from hymns of praise, the ones you're remembering now. Yes, the accompanying rituals are gone, but the power of the worshiping community is awakened in the oracle of comfort. Yahweh (not Marduk) created all this. God (not the king of Babylon) is in control.

One of the prominent themes of these hymns is the incomparability of God, a cultural trope that signifies the highest form of praise. To whom can you compare God? Who is God's equal? No other is like the One. This is a common biblical assertion, given expression in the common names Mi-ka-'el and Mi-ka-ya(hu) and Micah: "Who is like God/Yahweh?" It is found among the oldest poetry in the Bible, "Who is like you, O LORD, among the gods? / Who is like you,… / awesome in splendor?"(Ex. 15:11).

Incomparability is also related to ineffability. We know things only insofar as we can describe their likeness. So the use of this convention also expresses the ultimate mystery of God and acknowledges that our language and symbols can never adequately grasp the being and will of God. I was taught that pious believers do not pronounce the name of God, not because that name is too holy, but because we believers must avoid assuming that it is possible to grasp God, to fully understand God, or to control God.

Incomparability is also related, sometimes implicitly and sometimes explicitly, to the monotheistic claim that there are no other gods. There are no equals or even standards of measure that might be mustered to quantify God's greatness. Not the idols— even the skillfully made ones. Not the gods—even the beneficent ones. And certainly not the princes and rulers who like to play God—not even the powerful ones.

Having affirmed this, however, it is just as evident that the Bible is full of such implicit comparisons. While the effects of God's acts are described by explicit comparisons, or similes, God is always described metaphorically. God is a rock, a fortress, a redeemer/avenger of blood, a shepherd, a doting mother, a bridegroom, a warrior, a consuming fire, and a sound of sheer silence. A plethora of penultimate metaphors constitute the divine epithets of the Bible's prophetic and hymnic literature.

In this oracle of comfort the prophet uses the hymnic traditions of the pre-exilic temple to introduce the theme of Yahweh's sovereignty over nature and history. It contains a subtle polemic against the astral deities whose worship was at the heart of Babylonian religion. The assertion of God's sovereignty over the nations is intended to rouse the people from their stupor of lamentation and reestablish their faith.

Psalm 147 reflects some of the same themes as Isaiah's oracle of comfort. God's mighty works as Creator and Redeemer are rehearsed here from a postexilic perspective. God is a healer and a reverser of fortunes, a lifter of the downtrodden and a capsizer of the wicked. God takes note and takes care. The metaphors bring us into the vicinity of the great mystery. It is fitting to sing praise and give thanks to this God, for when we do this together, the community is reconstituted and sustained.

Finally, there are the characteristic aspects of God's delight and desire. This underappreciated and underutilized theological concept reflects a divine aesthetic that is deeply ethical. It belies the typical Christian images of the God of the so-called Old Testament as a wrathful, vengeful, punishing foil to the God and Father of our Lord Jesus Christ. Yahweh's delight is not in the strength of the horse or the speed of the runner, but in those who worship (fear) the One and hope in that loving loyalty.

This brings us back to the essential theme of Isaiah's comfort oracle. Those who wait and hope for Yahweh will be strengthened and renewed. These verbs denote not static inactivity, but active expectation. Those who wait, then, live in the faith that the God who created and sustains, who is incomparable, who overturns the plans of the most powerful princes of this world—that this God will do/is doing/has done the restorative and renewing work for child, woman, and man.

By worshiping its way to renewal and hope, the community of faith has something to offer a world full of weariness, faintness, powerlessness, and despair. Wherever the young are exhausted, wherever the old are clueless, those who know how to hope offer relief from pain and numbness with their songs of praise and joy.

Miracle Market

BARBARA CRAFTON

2 Kings 5:1–14; Mark 1:40–45

*Moved with pity, Jesus stretched out his hand and touched
him, and said to him, "I do choose. Be made clean!"
(Mark 1:41)*

An odd reticence marks the healings in the lessons for this
Sunday—an expectation of big-bang pyrotechnics is followed by
a matter-of-factness in the healings that seems to disappoint. The
haughty Naaman is downright offended by the simplicity of
Elisha's prescription for curing his leprosy. "I thought that for me
he would surely come out, and stand and call on the name of the
LORD his God, and would wave his hand over the spot" (2 Kings
5:11).

But nothing that glamorous is planned: Naaman should just
go and wash himself in the river. The river! As if he hadn't tried
washing before. As if the river Jordan were somehow a better river
than the great rivers of Syria, his own country. Naaman is like the
man in an old joke who is caught in a flood and goes up on the
roof, where he intends to wait for God to rescue him. Person after
person comes by in a rowboat, offering to take him to safety. "No,

thanks," he says. "I know God's going to save me." Finally the waters rise over him, and he dies. When he gets to heaven, he complains, "I prayed and prayed, but you didn't save me!" And God answers, "I sent four rowboats and you didn't get into any of them."

We don't claim the healings that come to us. Instead, we set the evidentiary bar so high for a miracle of healing that a dozen miracles happen to us and we don't notice any of them. For us, a miracle has to be magic, full of special effects, before we'll pay any attention. But most of the miracles we know are like rowboats. They come along regularly, but you have to get into them to get the full effect. When it comes to miracles, we are snobbish.

Who is it, after all, who encourages Naaman to go along with Elisha down to the river and wash, as the holy man has told him to do? His servants. Who persuades him to seek out Elisha, the famous holy man, in the first place? A little slave girl whom his soldiers had kidnapped from Israel. People without pretensions. People who have little to lose by looking foolish. People who know they don't count for much in the worldly scheme of things.

Here's the clue: there aren't special miracles for "important people." They don't heal differently from poor people. They are simply other brothers and sisters in pain and sorrow, and in sharing the same joy in Christ. The unimportant go first in the order of this kingdom, leading the way for the rest of us. The hierarchy of worldly privilege is gone, and blessings tumble abundantly over everyone.

Yet the reluctance to claim the miracles continues in the gospel reading from Mark. Here Jesus himself seems shy about what he has done. "Don't tell anyone," he warns the cleansed leper, but the man disobeys, and soon Jesus is on the run, hiding from the crowds. He draws back from the display of his power, even though his miracles are performed to show people that the kingdom is near.

Why? Is it because the people are not ready? Do they need to live through the weakness and despair of the end of Jesus' story on earth before they can be trusted with the fullness of his power? Perhaps they need to know the darkness before they can handle that light. It is the same with Christians today. Would we stick around to hear the whole story of who Jesus is if healing miracles were a common occurrence? Mightn't we just pick up our miracle and go home?

Even those closest to Jesus sometimes resembled Naaman. They had a hard time with the ordinariness of him, with his humiliation at the hands of a powerful and corrupt authority. He was the Christ, they agreed. But he ought to show his power more explicitly. He ought to show them who he was. "Save yourself! If you are the Son of God, come down from the cross" (Mt. 27:40), his enemies taunted him, and his friends wondered why he didn't do just that.

But would "showing" them his power have made the difference in Jesus' ministry? To claim a healing does not erase our humanness. The Jesus who healed people miraculously was also a person, and died in weakness. We claim a Jesus who is both God and human. Our faith and our human history walk through time together, and we can see God at work in the way faith and history influence each other.

Positive outcomes to problems do not certify the power of God except to those who read the story of humankind by the light of their faith. Believers are already disposed to see God's power at work. For the others, those who were alive when he walked the earth but who didn't claim the faith, Jesus' life must have looked like a failure. "Is that all?" some must have said. He seemed so promisingly powerful. "Was all that just destroyed? I'm glad I wasn't foolish enough to believe. Think how embarrassed I'd be now."

We see this power because we claim it, because, in a sense, we decide to see God at work. Someone heals spontaneously, or survives a difficult surgery, and sees a miracle. Someone dies on a cross, and the world sees failure and turns away. Others, however, glimpsed eternal life. They realized that they have a say in what they will accept and who they will follow.

Like them, we are not compelled by evidence. We are invited in, by faith.

Lame Excuse

BARBARA CRAFTON

Psalm 41; Isaiah 43:18–25; Mark 2:1–12

As for me, I said, "O LORD, be gracious to me;
heal me, for I have sinned against you." (Psalm 41:4)

People in Jesus' time thought that illness arose from people's sins. They thought this happened in a fairly immediate cause-and-effect relationship. And they had thought so for a long time. Many of the psalms, like Psalm 41, allude to the idea: "Heal me, for I have sinned against you."

Today we are more apt to think that illness afflicts us in a more random way. He "caught" a cold, we say; or he "developed" a tumor. In the story of his healing of the paralytic, Jesus seems to offer his hearers room for both approaches. "Your sins are forgiven," he tells the stricken man; and a collective murmur of shock and disbelief goes up from the crowd at his presumption in declaring forgiveness of sins. Who does this guy think he is? To clear things up, Jesus commands the paralytic to take up his bed and walk. The man gets up, picks up his pallet, and goes on home. Whether or not his malady arose from sin, the man is healed.

"See," says God to Isaiah, "I am doing a new thing. You thought you knew how the world works, but you know only so much. There are surprises in store for all of you, so stay tuned."

Many of the diseases that roamed the earth in ancient times, devastating all who crossed their paths, have now been tamed. Having conquered many of them, it seems that we will conquer all of them. Perhaps now we will have a world without illness, we think to ourselves. Then a new one comes along to terrify us. Still we have confidence: a cure is possible for anything if we just put enough research and enough money into finding it. And so we walk and bike and run for the cure. We give to the cancer society, the heart fund, and the diabetes foundation. We no longer give up on the sick, no longer isolate them, content to believe that they have brought their illness upon themselves. That's ancient history.

Or is it? We usually don't give up on the sick; we usually don't think they've brought it on themselves. But consider the history of the AIDS epidemic in this country and how it was veiled in secrecy and shame for ten years before we faced it as a public-health problem. Think of the euphemisms still employed in the newspaper obituaries when someone has died of HIV-related illness. And consider the devastation that secrecy continues to cause in Africa and Asia. For reasons of politics and public relations, government after government has refused to admit that AIDS was a problem in its country until it became almost insurmountable. The numbers are staggering: 40 percent of the adult populations of some African nations may be infected. Half the children may become orphans in the next five years, with no healthy adults left to care for them. Denial has proved fatal.

Or consider mental illnesses. The New Testament people assumed they were caused by demon possession. We don't think so today. Or do we? We still cloak these illnesses in shame and secrecy. When psychiatric illness grips its victims in behavior that isolates them and frightens those around them, we compound the misery by treating it like a failure of nerve or a character flaw. People are ashamed to admit they or someone they love has it, afraid someone will find out they're in therapy or that they take antidepressants—as if their illness were really a sin. And so they don't seek treatment, those who love them cannot understand their symptoms, and victims suffer for decades. Research on cures for mental illness lags far behind that for other illnesses in urgency and funding. There are no telethons for schizophrenia, although 2.2 million adults in America are afflicted, compared with the 250,000 who live with muscular dystrophy, another incurable disease. But the Jerry Lewis Telethon raised $58,000,000 for muscular dystrophy in 2001 alone.

Jesus couldn't have healed the paralytic if the man's friends hadn't been part of the project. He wouldn't have known about him. They had to work to get in to see Jesus: the door was blocked with onlookers, and they had to come in through the roof. We think of ourselves, of our caution, of our careful attitude toward our own longing for healing: we don't get our hopes up. What did they know that we don't know? What did they know that made them think this would work, that Jesus could do something new in this man's life? They must have been pretty sure, or they wouldn't have stuck their necks out like that.

Or pretty desperate.

Maybe. But I think it was this: they loved their friend a lot. They hated what his illness and pain was doing to him. Love was the force that propelled them forward into such extreme action. It made them brave—foolish, some of the onlookers might have said, but brave.

The Son of God is not yes and no, St. Paul says. In him it has always been yes. We may not think God sends heart disease or cancer to people because of their sins. We no longer charge God with the "no" in human history. But we do look to God for the "yes." We do know that God sends patient caregivers, dedicated researchers and physicians, devoted family and friends to walk with the ill through their painful journey, whether it be a journey toward cure or a journey toward a fuller life. Such people are sent from God whether they know it or not. Anyone who is part of the "yes"—part of the healing, the comfort, the building-up—is a servant of God.

Time Out of Time

PATRICK WILLSON

Mark 9:2–9

As he came down from the mountain of the transfiguration with his disciples, Jesus commanded them to tell no one what they had seen "until after the Son of Man [has] risen from the dead" (Mk. 9:9c). When they did begin to speak about what had happened on the mountain, they must have discovered the wisdom of Jesus' admonition. Indeed, one suspects that this is when the expression, "Well, I suppose you had to be there" might have been born. No matter what we say about the transfiguration, we never quite seem able to explain it.

A century ago it was fashionable to account for it in terms of natural phenomena. On a snowcapped mountain Jesus encountered a pair of men dressed in white robes. The glare of the sun reflected on their garments by the snow was so dazzling that the disciples thought…When we try to untangle the transfiguration, often the explanations begin sounding even more improbable than the gospel story itself.

Recent excavations in literary archaeology have suggested that the transfiguration is a misplaced resurrection story. The white robes, resplendent light and transformed personages make that sound reasonable enough. Some have gone so far as to identify the story as a refugee from the apocryphal gospel of Peter; after wandering from church to church, the story finally found a canonical home in the middle of Mark's gospel. But why would Mark, whose avoidance of resurrection accounts is both infamous and problematic, insert an Easter story at the midpoint of his gospel?

Like Peter, we use whatever tools we have at hand to come to terms with the transfiguration. If the idea of hammering together three booths and enclosing the event within the celebration of Sukkoth suggests that Peter was straining to find a fit for what he had witnessed, surely we can be sympathetic. Mark gently explains that the apostle really didn't know what to say. Nothing in our experience prepares us for what Mark describes. Nowhere among the notions by which we order our lives is there a category in which the transfiguration might "fit." It does not even fit particularly well into Mark's gospel. Until this point, Mark has maintained a frenetic pace, portraying Jesus as moving "immediately" from task to task—casting out a demon, healing Simon Peter's mother-in-law, teaching, telling a paralytic to take up his pallet and walk. Jesus' story is narrated with furious intensity.

Now, on the mountaintop, time evaporates like mist before the dawning of a great glory. If the pace of the journey has left us panting, now the height is too great for us to catch our breath. This is not just one more story among many. This is not just another moment following in the sequence of events. Here on the mountain, time is abandoned for a moment of eternity.

Though some speak of the transfiguration as a theophany, what irrupts is not some offstage *deus ex machina,* but the Christus Victor who invades time from his throne at the end of time. What is revealed on the mountain is not who Jesus is but what he will be. Elijah appears as the harbinger of the messianic reign, Moses as an eschatological figure of royalty; together they verify the enthronement of Jesus as the Christ of God. This transfiguring event occurs out of season, however, in the time of "not yet."

Jesus has predicted his rejection, suffering, and death, and summoned those who would follow him to "take up their cross" (8:31–34). But how can anyone face such an undertaking without a meaningful vision of where it will lead? Mark does not point to a happy ending in these early chapters of his gospel. But to his congregation, themselves rejected, suffering, and facing death, he hints of a vision of rejection, suffering, and death transfigured in unimaginable glory. There will be a time for a *theologia gloria,* but that time is "not yet." The fulfillment of all things has a way of overflowing its banks and invading our time.

J. R. R. Tolkien distinguishes between different kinds of climaxes. The tragic tale, with its sorrowful ending, he calls a "dyscatastrophe"; for "the Consolation of the Happy Ending" he coined the word "eucatastrophe": the blessed cataclysm by which lovers are reunited after many tests and trials, or the true king is separated from all pretenders and finally ascends the throne. "In such stories," Tolkien says, "when the sudden 'turn' comes we get a piercing glimpse of joy, and heart's desire, that for a moment passes outside the frame, rends indeed the very web of the story, and lets a gleam come through." Mark's "eucatastrophe" cracks open his story at midpoint, leaving us stunned and speechless. Like Peter, we press into service whatever transformations, transmutations, or transmogrifications we have known, clumsily likening them to what we have glimpsed on the mountain. We say what we can say and wait "until after the Son of Man [be] risen from the dead."

Test Run

FRED CRADDOCK

Mark 1:9–15

> *He was in the wilderness forty days, tempted by Satan; and he*
> *was with the wild beasts; and the angels waited on him.*
> *(Mark 1:13)*

It is difficult to listen to a text when other texts are in the room talking about the same subject matter, often in ways more elaborate and more familiar. Mark is the text before us, but Matthew, Luke, and John are also in the room. Each has a right to be heard, and there are times when it is profitable to entertain them all at once, noting differences and wondering why. But for the present, Mark is speaking; courtesy and respect demand that we pay attention to him.

Even when listening to one text, it is remarkable how many echoes of other voices can be heard. Most texts are layered, tradition upon tradition, and from those layers come instruction and enrichment. To be sure, the text being read carries its own sense and sufficient clarity. One does not have to know Exodus, Kings, Psalms, Isaiah, and Malachi to find satisfaction in reading Mark 1:1–15, just as one does not need to know Shakespeare to appreciate John Steinbeck's *Winter of Our Discontent,* or Ezra Pound to follow Adela Rogers St. Johns's *The Honeycomb.* But how much fuller and richer the experience when one does! Reading Mark is a blessing; reading Mark aware of his rich resources is a double, a triple blessing.

Now to Mark 1:9–15. The writer, with almost shocking brevity, relates three major events: Jesus' baptism, temptation in the desert, and first preaching in Galilee. The sequence of events is significant, not simply because it seems the natural order of things, but because in a new exodus Jesus recapitulates the journey of Israel: baptism (Red Sea), struggles in the desert (forty years), and good news (entry into the promised land). In a similar move, Paul drew a parallel between the Corinthian church's experience of baptism, table fellowship, and temptations, and Israel's baptism in the sea, sharing of God-given food and drink, and temptations in the desert (1 Cor. 10:1–13). The texts and the experiences of God's people unfold, layer upon layer.

Let's attend to Jesus' temptation in the desert. Notice how aware of the reader the narrative is. In an account in which only Satan, wild animals, and angels are with Jesus, the reader is also present. This is no historical reporting with all the proper distance of objectivity; the reader is drawn in to hear, to see, to experience. Such is the way of scripture to make its message present to the one who reads. The reader is on Mount Moriah where only Abraham and Isaac are talking. The reader is on the Mount of Transfiguration where only Jesus, Peter, James, and John experience God. The reader is with Jesus in Gethsemane while the apostles sleep, and in Pilate's chambers as he and Jesus talk privately. The reader is close enough to the cross to overhear Jesus speak to his mother and the beloved disciple. Questions of historical accuracy may be raised, but not here, not now.

Notice also the vigor of the language when the subject is testing or temptation. Immediately after receiving the Spirit at baptism, Jesus is driven by the Spirit into the desert. Clearly God is at work here, but so is the adversary, Satan. Forty days the struggle continues. Jesus is in the company of wild animals, and angels "waited on him," that is, served him food. It is unclear whether Mark has in mind the pre-fall state of Adam when wild animals were as yet no threat, or the post-fall state in which wild animals were a danger to the expelled Adam. Since the scene before us is one of struggle, very likely the wild animals and the angels represent the two forces battling with Jesus. Whatever the ancient echoes, it is clear that Jesus is not on a pensive evening walk in the desert; he is being tested intensely.

Mark does not elaborate on the temptation. So what is happening? Obviously, Jesus was really being tempted. There is no need to protect Jesus by saying he only seemed to be tempted to set us an example. Anyone who pretends an experience to set an example is not setting an example. "We have one who in every respect has been tested as we are, yet without sin" (Heb. 4:15b). Nor should one rob the event of its reality on the assumption that temptation is weakness. We are not tempted to do what we cannot do but what we can. The testing is one of strength, and the stronger, the more capable, the greater one is, the greater the temptation. As George Buttrick once said in a sermon, "You do not have a sea storm in a roadside puddle."

And if the temptation is real, it most certainly is deceptive. Temptation is not obvious, definitely not a caricature: "Hi, I am Satan; I am here to tempt you." The tempter often looks and sounds like a friend or relative. "Get behind me, Satan!" was not Jesus' word to the local fiend but to his friend, Simon Peter. At the heart of the deception are offers not to fall but to rise. The tempter in Eden did not ask, "Do you wish to be as the devil?" but "Do you wish to be as God?" "If you are really the Son of God…," says the voice in Jesus' mind. There is nothing here of the debauchery often associated with temptation. No self-respecting Satan would approach a person with offers of personal, social, and professional ruin. That is in the small print at the bottom of the temptation.

Still wet from his baptism, Jesus struggles, apparently, with the burden that lies within the words, "You are my Son, the Beloved; with you I am well pleased."

Lenten Roadmap

FRED CRADDOCK

Romans 4:13–25

The life situation of the reader of a text provides a lens through which that text is read. Or, to change the metaphor, the life situation provides the magnet, which draws from a text that which most clearly addresses the reader. For the same reader the same text may, under different circumstances, console or correct or convict or enlighten or inspire. If this is true of one reader, then certainly a nursing home resident and a teenager at camp do not read the same way. This observation is neither an endorsement of total relativity nor a reduction of the text to an inkblot test. (What do you see? I see an elephant. I see an airplane.) Rather, it is to recognize how the Bible functions as scripture; that is, how it speaks an appropriate word. As a document of the past, the text is at home in the hands of historians. As the scripture of the church, the text is at home in the inquiring faith of believers.

We are reading Romans 4:13–25 with the eyes of believers on a Lenten journey to Jerusalem. By a Lenten journey we mean a time of reflection, repentance, and preparation for arrival at Good Friday and Easter. Under other circumstances this text might revive in us the debate over law and gospel, works and grace.

There is a proper time and place for that, but not now. Now we are instructed and nourished by the striking affirmation about "the God in whom he [Abraham] believed, who gives life to the dead and calls into existence the things that do not exist" (Rom. 4:17b). This statement reminds us that God is both the subject and the object of faith. As the subject of faith, God initiates faith. God called Abraham; God promised Abraham. Here faith begins and is sustained. And the one who believes is responding to and trusting in the God who calls and promises.

How refreshing to speak of and think of God! In the church we often hear of Christ and the Holy Spirit, but we only sometimes hear of God. Of course, Christ and the Holy Spirit are appropriate and essential subjects in Christian worship, preaching and teaching, but God sent the Son Jesus Christ and the Holy Spirit. All things, says Paul, are from God, through God, and to God (Rom. 11:36). "Show us the Father, and we will be satisfied," says Philip on behalf of the whole human race (John 14:8). Many churches seem to assume that everyone already believes in God and that what we need is the addition of Christ. Not so. "Do you believe in God?" is the appropriate first question.

Romans 4:17 not only instructs us but also nourishes us by its characterization of God as one "who gives life to the dead." The additional expression, "and calls into existence the things that do not exist," is not intended as a lead-in to another line of thinking. Paul is not entering into the debate about whether creation is out of nothing rather than out of some primordial mass. Rather, Paul is affirming that God gives life to the dead in the sense that God gives life and being where there were none before (see verses 18–25).

The God who gives life to the dead is revealed in the stories of certain people. Abraham's Sarah was barren and far past child-bearing years. In this respect their lineage was "dead," and yet God had promised Abraham descendants in multitudes. Abraham hoped in the face of hopelessness. He was convinced that God was able to do what he had promised, and held on tenaciously to the creed behind all creeds: Nothing is impossible with God. And Abraham's faith was rewarded: all who trust in God, both Jew and Gentile, are children of Abraham. God, indeed, gave life to the dead.

Jesus Christ: Jesus was dead, no question about that. Ask the soldiers, the Galilean women who followed him to Golgotha, Mary his mother. For some, of course, that death was too much to accept, too final, too contrary to hopes stirred. Desperation spun theories: Simon of Cyrene who bore the cross for him was crucified by mistake. A potion given to Jesus on the cross sent him into a deathlike slumber. His immortal soul ascended above the cross, leaving behind a corpse that was no longer Jesus. The theories are endless. But the church would have none of it: "He suffered under Pontius Pilate, was crucified, dead, and buried." On the third day, God gave life to the dead.

The believer: buried in the phrases "trespasses" and "our justification" is the drama of the death and resurrection not only of Christ but also of the believer. Paul seems not to favor the image of "born again" but prefers instead to speak of coming to faith as being made alive. "Even when we were dead through our trespasses, [God] made us alive together with Christ—by grace you have been saved—and raised us up with him" (Eph. 2:5–6a). Paul applied such thinking to baptism: death, burial and resurrection with Christ (Rom. 6:3–4). God's act in Abraham, and in Jesus Christ, is brought home as an unfailing reality in the believer: God gives life to the dead.

For the one who believes in the God who gives life to the dead, the Lenten journey is not only to Good Friday and Easter, but is also a revisiting of one's own experience. Belief in this intersection of theology, christology, and experience makes the traveler through Lent a pilgrim. Without this faith one is simply a tourist. Bring your camera; there may be camels.

Life-giving Law

FRED CRADDOCK

Psalm 19

Lent carries in its bosom a seductive danger: excessive inwardness. The seduction is this: a season of prayer, repentance, and preparation for Good Friday and Easter necessarily involves trips to the heart, but tarry there too long and repentance can stall out as melancholy. The danger is this: self-examination may spawn attempts at self-improvement, with the result that looking at self replaces looking to God, and small measures of merit replace the immeasurable grace of God. One can hardly imagine a more effective shield against this danger than Psalm 19.

Notice the size of this text: it moves from the revelation of God in heavens, sky, and sun (vv. 1–6) to the revelation of God in sacred scripture (vv. 7–10) to the mysterious working of God's word in the mind and heart of the believer (vv. 11–14). Notice the mood of this text: the writer is not self-absorbed but is fully engaged in the praise of God, pausing briefly to express the hope that the worship will be accepted. Notice the community involvement: the antiphonal form of most of this psalm makes it clear that a choir and congregation, or at least two groups in a worship assembly, are participating, rather than an individual in private. Note the energy: unlike a pensive reflection, Psalm 19 pulsates with verbs of activity: telling, proclaiming, pouring forth, declaring, going out, running, rising, reviving, making wise, rejoicing, enlightening, enduring. This is not to say that this text breaks or violates the basic orientation of Lent. On the contrary, nothing could be more appropriate than this vigorous contemplation of God.

The psalmist begins by walking outside and reading the face of creation as though it were an open book. Creation awes the observer with its revelation of God. As Paul would say, "Ever since the creation of the world his eternal power and divine nature, invisible though they are, have been understood and seen through the things he has made" (Rom. 1:20). Or Luke: "He has not left himself without a witness in doing good—giving you rains from heaven and fruitful seasons, and filling you with food and your hearts with joy" (Acts 14:16–17).

Whose heart has not joined the psalmist and Paul and Luke in this chorus of praise to the Creator? Who has not in spring, when the world is a poem of light and color, delighted in the meadows turning somersaults of joy and "butterflies fluttering up from every little buttercup"? Or in dry hot summer, when clouds dark and heavy gather on the hill, soon thundering like a herd of buffalo across the valley, making glad the gardens and sending out the children to splash in the puddles? Or in the autumn with leaves aflame, poised between summer and winter, warm enough but yet prophetic of snow? Or in the winter when trees now shivering naked beg heaven for a blanket and down it comes thick and white, turning even a garbage can into an altar in praise of God? There is no square inch of earth so barren that the observing eye cannot see, in the lower right-hand corner, the signature of the artist. And overhead the stars sing and faith hears faintly the rustle of a wing.

But it is not enough. The great book of nature praises the Creator without words, but its pages have no answers for some fundamental human questions. Whence do we come? Whither do we go? Why are we here? Before these questions the stars can only flicker and the mockingbird forgets its song. We need another book.

The psalmist knows this, and turns his attention to another book, the law of the Lord (vv. 7–10). It is important to remember that "law" is a Greek translation of Torah, a translation that implies "legal code," the basis for Paul's development of his law vs. grace arguments in Galatians and Romans. However, law is but one element of Torah. Torah is the first five books of the scriptures, and includes history, biography, story, and poetry, as well as law. The Jewish worshiper delights in Torah and reflects on it continually.

The psalmist uses six nouns to try to capture this many-splendored thing: law, decrees, precepts, commandment, fear (reverence), and ordinances. No single verb conveys its activity, so he uses five: reviving, making wise, rejoicing, enlightening, enduring. And seven adjectives: perfect, sure, right, clear, pure, true, righteous. Unlike nature, this book recalls the shadowy beginning of God's people: slavery, deliverance, wandering, revelation of God's will for the faithful community, and bright promise in the land. In this book is nourishment enough to spare. In this book is the offer of identity, security, discipline, and direction. Finer than gold, sweeter than honey is Torah.

Then comes the inescapable thought: the benefits of Torah belong not to the one who reads, and not even to the one who reads and admires, but to the one who follows it. The eye that scanned the heavens and read the book now turns nervously inward (vv. 11–4). Critical self-examination brings two painful revelations: faults that are proud, even arrogant, strutting openly and defiant, in full view of all; and faults buried so deep in the heart that even the transgressor is unaware of them. But God knows. As nothing is hidden from the sun, so nothing is hidden from God.

The worshiper's journey is complete: from the broad reaches of God's creation through the guiding lines of scripture to the disturbing inner recesses of the heart, there remains only the prayer. May the God praised with and without speech find acceptable the words and thoughts of the worshiper. Only then can one join creation and scripture in the endless adoration of God.

From God to God

FRED CRADDOCK

Ephesians 2:1–10

And [God] raised us up with [Christ] and seated us with him
in the heavenly places in Christ Jesus. (Ephesians 2:6)

In Dallas, Texas, one week prior to the assassination of President
Kennedy, I heard German New Testament scholar Joachim
Jeremias reminisce about his life in Israel, where his parents were
missionaries. After WWII, he returned nervously to Israel to see
if the treatment of Jews by the Nazi regime had severed forever
his friendships there. When he knocked at the door of an old friend,
he was welcomed with an embrace. He joined his friend in the
backyard, where a crude tent had been erected for the observance
of the Feast of Tents or Booths, a time of recalling Israel's
wandering in the desert, dwelling in tents. Fastened on the
entrance to the tent were two slips of paper, each bearing a brief
message: on the left was "From God"; on the right was "To God."
There, simply yet dramatically, said Jeremias, was the whole of
life: from God, to God, and in the years between, a tent.

His recollection is a commentary on Ephesians 2:1–10; or, more
correctly, on Ephesians 1:3—3:20. Ephesians 1—3 is widely

regarded as a baptismal liturgy, or at least a portion of one. How appropriate that the church prepare candidates for baptism during Lent! What most needs to be impressed on the candidate on the occasion of being set apart for God and God's service in a world confused and estranged from its Creator? One could do for the baptismal candidate what the writer of Ephesians does for the reader, that is, interpret what is happening to a person entering the Christian life. To "interpret" is not to enter the classroom for an academic exercise; interpreting is a common and necessary activity of every community. It is what a parent does when a child asks, "What is that noise?" or "Do hamsters go to heaven?" It is what a physician does when a patient worries about numbness in the left arm or intense headaches. Teachers do it, as do lawyers, friends, spouses, and neighbors. As do churches. In fact, interpreting is a primary activity of the church and its leaders. "What does it mean," asks the candidate, "to become a Christian?"

The Ephesians text answers the question experientially. The language is vivid: You were dead. This is to say, you were caught in a futile way of life obedient to desires of the flesh, seeking the approval of your culture, heeding every inclination that led away from God, aimless and helpless to extricate yourself. But God, rich in love and mercy, by free unmerited favor, quickened your life and set you in a safe place in the constant presence of Christ. You are now alive, but not simply to enjoy God's grace. You have been created again as God's masterpiece for two purposes: to show what God can do through Jesus Christ, and to serve human need, engaging in good works that reflect the nature of God as gracious love.

The Ephesians text answers the question historically. As unexciting as this may sound, it must never be overlooked. Israel has a history, Jesus has a history, and the church has a history. To be a Christian is to enter into that history, to say we were in Egypt, we were in Nazareth, we were in Jerusalem, Rome, Geneva, Wittenberg, and Boston. But the primary historical location of the believer, according to Ephesians 2:5-6, is Jesus Christ. The text does not use the usual Pauline phrase "in Christ Jesus," but "with Christ Jesus." The historical references to him are brief but sufficient: he was crucified, he died, he was buried, he was raised, and he was enthroned. To be a Christian, says the text, is to be crucified with Jesus, to die with him, to be buried with him, to be raised with him, to be enthroned with him. Spiritual? Yes.

Mystical? Perhaps. Subjective? Partially. Will-o'-the-wisp? Never. Experiential but inseparable from history? Always.

Finally, the Ephesians text answers the question "What does it mean to enter the Christian life?" by setting the believer in a cosmic context. Spatially, this context extends from "this world" to "the heavenly places." This represents what the Greeks called *ta panta*, the totality. The totality included the subterranean region, the earth, and the heavens, and in every place, says Paul, dwelt hostile powers, including "the ruler of the power of the air." and "the rulers and authorities in the heavenly places" (3:10). For all their power to cripple, control, and alienate, all hostilities in the universe will not only cease ultimately, but will be reconciled. For redemption in Christ to be complete, it must range as far and wide as the forces of evil. And his liberating work has already begun in setting free the person caught in the passions of the senses and enamored of this world's offerings. Change the world view, change the language, and any adequate interpretation of the Christian life must still range this far.

Temporally, the cosmic context for the Christian life extends from "the foundation of the world" (Eph. 1:4), that which "God prepared beforehand" (2:10), to "the age to come" (1:21). Many, of course, do not think in terms of before time and after time, and they seem to function without this concept. But what such language seeks to convey is hardly a casual option. The life of the believer is set in a narrative far grander than the narrow parentheses of one lifetime. Faith says there is a metanarrative, a story within which our stories make sense. In other words, "from God, to God."

Jesus the Priest

FRED CRADDOCK

Hebrews 5:5–10

*So also Christ did not glorify himself in becoming a high
priest, but was appointed by the one who said to him,
"You are my Son,
    today I have begotten you." (Hebrews 5:5)*

The letter to the Hebrews joins the Revelation to John as the
literature most intimidating to readers of the New Testament. With
the Revelation the reader must endure its terrible splendor; with
Hebrews the reader must listen intently to the tightly woven
arguments in what the writer calls a sermon. No question about
it, the listening is demanding, not only because of the writer's
rhetorical style but also because of the assumption that the reader
knows the Old Testament and the wilderness life of Israel, a life
centered in the tabernacle and the daily ministrations of the priest.
The difficulty for the reader is softened, however, by the realization
that the writer is fully aware of the burden. For example, after
introducing the "M" word, *Melchizedek*, the writer relaxes the
reader with "about this we have much to say that is hard to

explain" (Heb. 5:11a), and then does not return to the theme until Hebrews 7:1. The recess is welcome.

In fact, the style of the writer is patient and pastoral; the path is cleared for primary themes. For instance, the author focuses the sermon on the affirmation that Christ's saving work is that of a priest. Obviously such a view will draw not "amens," but questions. Jesus was no priest! He was of the tribe of Judah, not Levi. When did he serve at the altar or perform the sacred rites? He cleansed the temple with a whip and clashed with the priests. How can one claim he was a priest? Into such an unusual thought the reader must be led patiently. And so, Jesus as priest is only implied in 1:3b, briefly stated in 2:17, presented more strongly in 3:1, elaborated upon with great pastoral warmth in 4:14–16, and finally developed at length with both reason and scripture beginning at 5:1. The writer pauses at 5:11 to say, "I know this is difficult." How considerate of the reader Hebrews is!

Before arguing that Jesus belongs to an order of priests prior to and different from the Levitical priesthood, the author addresses the fundamental questions: Who is a priest? What does a priest do? These questions are answered briefly but clearly. A priest represents God to the people in words and actions. The distance implied when we speak of the transcendence of God is negotiated through the ministries of the priest, and the people before the altar experience the word and the presence of God. Obviously, no one would presume to take this role upon himself or herself. Being a priest is not simply one's "chosen profession," as though taking the training and putting on the robes made one a priest. A priest is of God, God chosen, God appointed. The writer assumes there is no need to argue the point.

But does Jesus qualify? Beyond question, says our text. He was appointed by the God who had said, "You are my Son," and words from coronation Psalm 2 declaring that the Son is also King. That same God now says of the Son-King, "You are a priest forever" (Ps. 110:4). Nothing further is said. For the community of faith, Jesus Christ is appointed priest forever, like Melchizedek, without beginning or end (Hebrews 7:1–10).

However, the picture is not yet complete, for a priest must not only be of God but also of the people. He must become like his brothers and sisters in every respect, tested through suffering in order to help those being tested (2:17–18). Only then can the priest deal gently with the ignorant and wayward (5:2). The ministries of a true priest are performed in full sympathy with the people.

Again, does Jesus qualify? The answer is yes, but it is not an easy yes. That Jesus was of God was a swift affirmation, needing the support of only two brief quotations from the psalms; that Jesus was of the people seems to call for repetition and elaboration.

Jesus...

was made for a little while lower than the angels (2:9);

was not ashamed to call us brother and sister (2:11);

shared with us flesh and blood (2:14);

is able to sympathize with our weaknesses, having been tested as we are, yet without sin, and therefore able to offer mercy and grace in time of need (4:14–16).

One would think these statements are enough to complete satisfactorily the ancient Christian formula: he was not as we are and therefore can help; he was as we are and therefore will help.

Yet it seems that the writer feels he cannot say often enough that Christ was and is one with the people. It is as though there were in the writer himself or in the reader a caution, a hesitation about this article of our faith, that Christ was "truly human." Therefore this quality, essential for any priest, is declared once more, not with quotations from scripture, not with bold pronouncements, but with a scene from the earthly life of the historical Jesus, or as the writer puts it, "in the days of his flesh." "Jesus offered up prayers and supplications, with loud cries and tears, to the one who was able to save him from death, and he was heard because of his reverent submission" (5:7).

This passage raises the tantalizing question of whether the writer was familiar with the gospel tradition about Jesus, and with Gethsemane. But of greater importance is the author's inclusion of the life of Jesus in the message we call "the gospel." The death, burial, and resurrection of Jesus are not all we need to know. And the point in his life that most vividly touches our own, qualifying him to be our priest, is his time of fervent prayer. His kneeling beside us as we offer up loud cries and tears is already an answer to prayer.

Protest March

FRED CRADDOCK

Mark 11:1–11

Then those who went ahead and those who followed were
shouting,
"Hosanna!
    Blessed is the one who comes in the name of the Lord!"
(Mark 11:9)

Even if we've set out on the Lenten pilgrimage on Ash Wednesday and taken every step in penitence and prayer, we are still not prepared for the arrival. Neither were those who joined Jesus in Galilee and made their way up to Jerusalem. For many it was an annual pilgrimage, this Passover. Others, having to travel greater distances, saw the Holy City through the joyful tears of those who know they will never make the journey again. But in one particular year, the pilgrimage was a once-in-a-lifetime experience because it was made in the company of Jesus of Nazareth. For him, too, Jerusalem was the end of a pilgrimage.

The portion of the journey to which Mark draws our attention goes from Bethany, a town just east of the Mount of Olives, to Jerusalem. It is difficult to listen to Mark describe the scene because the event has been elevated into a major Christian celebration, Palm Sunday or Passion Sunday, and celebrations tend to draw upon all the available resources to enlarge the drama. Matthew contributes the children, John the palms, and all the evangelists except Mark describe the pilgrimage as going into the streets of the city. Only Mark speaks of the procession going to the entrance of the city, and says that Jesus went alone into Jerusalem. He alone enters the temple, not to occupy it, not to cleanse it, but to survey it, and then to leave it and the city, retiring with the Twelve to Bethany. Simply put, Mark's account is not only brief, it is restrained and without the claims about Jesus found in the other three gospels.

This is not to say that the journey from Bethany to Jerusalem is for Mark an unimpressive parade. There is the mysterious locating and commandeering of an unbroken colt, the silence of Jesus except for instruction to two disciples, the large and loud crowd, the garments and branches to pave his way, and the bursts of praise and blessing. But this description is subdued compared to that of Matthew, who makes Zechariah 9:9 the centerpiece of the event, calls Jesus King, says the people hailed Jesus as Son of David, enlarges the crowd, and pictures all Jerusalem in turmoil over the celebration. The relatively modest narrative in Mark is consonant with the secrecy surrounding Jesus throughout this gospel. The popular description "triumphal entry" better fits Matthew than Mark, and neither gospel justifies the church's celebration of the day as though it were an Easter before Easter. As we sometimes have early warm weather called "false spring," so it is possible to observe a "false Easter." Those who keep the last Sunday of Lent as Passion rather than as Palm Sunday avoid the problem.

Whatever may have been in the minds of the crowds, whatever may have been in the minds of the Twelve, the reader knows something more is going on than a parade honoring Jesus. One might describe the event as a protest march. Although there is only a dramatic hint of protest in the passage before us—he entered the temple, looked around and left—the larger context justifies the term. While still in Galilee, Jesus had engaged Pharisees and scribes in serious disagreement over the interpretation of scripture and tradition. In addition to the running debate over table fellowship, sharp differences arose over fasting and Sabbath observance. Jesus protested the subordination of human need and welfare to the rigid and unfeeling application of law. As early as chapter three, Mark reports that Jesus' positions on key issues brought threats against his life. And, of course, once Jesus was in Jerusalem, protest followed protest, beginning with Jesus' interference with temple practices.

The stakes are higher now—he is no longer in the villages and open country of his home province. This is the capital and the seat of religious and civil authority, where chief priests and elders have power. To what extent the crowds of pilgrims or the residents of Jerusalem supported his protests is not fully clear. The crowds were "spellbound by his teaching," and Jesus' popularity with them caused his opponents to fear the crowds.

The final Sunday of Lent is therefore marked by a celebratory parade, which was also a protest march. Only Jesus knew that the same event was also a funeral procession. The Twelve should have known; on three occasions Jesus had told them of his approaching death in Jerusalem. Their response after each prediction makes it evident, however, that they did not comprehend his words. It is painful to read of their continuing claims of adequacy for what lies ahead and of their divisive competition for seats of favor in the coming kingdom.

But we must not rush to judgment. The Twelve spent much time with Jesus listening and observing, it is true, but that time together lay on the other side of the cross and the empty tomb. After the resurrection they remembered—and for the first time, they understood. To their credit, they regrouped. Records subsequent to Mark testify to faithfulness in continuing the work of Jesus, even in the face of opposition as strong as any Jesus himself had to endure.

It is important for the reader to remember that we know the end of the story and view the whole through an empty tomb. This realization checks our impatience with those who walked with him from the Mount of Olives to Jerusalem. But this realization is also a burden, a burden of knowing. How solemn and heavy is the joy of being admitted into the circle of those who now understand, at least in part. "To whom much is given…"

He Is Not Here

FRED CRADDOCK

Mark 16:1–8

> *But he said to them, "Do not be alarmed; you are looking for Jesus of Nazareth, who was crucified. He has been raised; he is not here. Look, there is the place they laid him." (Mark 16:6)*

We will have to deal with the question sooner or later, so we might as well get it over with: Where does the gospel of Mark end? There are four possibilities. The ending with the least support among ancient Greek manuscripts of Mark is the one comprising 16:8 and a short summary statement. This "shorter ending" is obviously non-Markan. The longest ending, verse 8 plus verses 9–20 plus a lengthy insert, is also suspect (the insert after verse 14 is especially lacking in manuscript support). The third candidate, verse 8 plus verses 9–20 without the insert, has more manuscript support, but the verses are not in the oldest and most reliable texts of Mark, and some of them are found in the other three gospels and Acts. These verses can best be read as the work of a Christian scribe seeking to overcome the awkwardness of ending at verse 8.

That leaves Mark 16:1–8, with its awkward Easter ending. "They said nothing to anyone, for they were afraid" is hardly a shout of victory over death. There is no appearance of the risen Christ to the women or anyone else. In the Greek text the final word in verse 8 is "for." Granted, this is a conjunction, which in Greek is not normally placed at the beginning of a clause, but even so it is an unusual final word in a narrative. Some scholars are convinced that the original ending, being the outermost part of a scroll, was worn off or broken off. Our task is to accept this text as Mark's Easter account and to hear what it says and does not say.

Following a death, there is nothing to do, and there is much to do. There is nothing to do: nobody goes to work, nobody goes to school, nobody is hungry, nobody has anything to say. Helpers are helpless, and in the way. There is much to do: legal matters need attention, the body must be prepared for burial, a tomb must be located. Fortunately for the family and friends of Jesus, a nearby tomb has been provided by one Joseph of Arimathea, who himself placed the corpse in the tomb and rolled a stone against the door. Mark does not indicate that the body was prepared with spices since the burial was in haste, the sabbath day being very near. However, two Galilean women, Mary Magdalene and Mary the mother of James, saw what Joseph did, and came after the Sabbath, along with Salome, to anoint the body.

What happened at the tomb is told in five verses. The stone has been rolled away, a young man in white (an angel?) is seated inside on the right, and—as would be expected when experiencing a divine revelation—the women are alarmed. The Easter message they receive is brief: do not be afraid; Jesus was crucified; he was placed here; he is not here now because he has been raised. Then they receive an Easter commission: go, tell his disciples and Peter that Jesus is going ahead of them to Galilee; in Galilee they will see him. This is the message Jesus had told them earlier. The response of the women is to run in terror, amazement, fear, and silence.

Is this any way to run a resurrection? Is this enough to persuade, to stir new life in the followers of Jesus? First, let it be said that none of the gospels provides an unambiguous, totally convincing account. Matthew says the disciples worshiped Jesus but some doubted; Luke says that in their joy they were disbelieving; and John says one of the Twelve refused to believe until he touched and felt. Faith is not coerced, even on Easter. In the New Testament, faith is response to divine revelation, and Mark provides that from the mouth of the young man in the tomb.

Second, Mark did not need an appearance of the risen Christ to affirm his faith in the resurrection. Faith can be expressed by adding an appearance after death and burial, or it can be expressed by remembrance of Jesus' repeated promise of a resurrection. Mark chose the latter. Descending the Mount of Transfiguration, he told Peter, James, and John not to speak of their experience until after the resurrection. Each of the three predictions of the passion included a prediction of resurrection; and on the way to Gethsemane, Jesus said, "But after I am raised up, I will go before you to Galilee" (Mk. 14:28). At the tomb the angel said to tell his disciples and Peter that he would meet them in Galilee, "just as he told you." The recollection of the words of Jesus is the stuff of faith.

Third, the question of why Mark, who obviously believed in the resurrection, included no appearance of the risen Christ is a natural one raised by the text itself. We can only speculate, but a reasonable answer may lie in Mark's accent on the cross. He has told the story of Jesus from baptism to crucifixion. The journey to Jerusalem was a journey to the cross, and all who would follow him must take up the cross. Perhaps for Mark, ending the story with a glorious resurrection would have reduced the cross to a stop on the way to resurrection and have turned the tomb cave into a tunnel with light shining through. Perhaps.

Fourth, even Mark's brief Easter account is full of good news. To disciples who had abandoned him and to Peter who denied him, Jesus' word was, "I will meet you in Galilee. There we began together; there we will begin anew."

And finally, of the women, afraid and silent: what can be said? When such persons find their voices, what powerful witnesses! No glib and easy Easter words here. They had been to the cemetery.

No Joke

Kristen Bargeron Grant

John 20:19–31; Acts 4:32–35

When it was evening on that day, the first day of the week,
and the doors of the house where the disciples had met were
locked for fear of the Jews, Jesus came and stood among them
and said, "Peace be with you." (John 20:19)

In the poem "Manifesto: The Mad Farmer Liberation Front," Wendell Berry's mad farmer warns against the love of "the quick profit, the annual raise, vacation with pay," a life that makes one "afraid to know your neighbors and to die." Instead, the mad farmer exhorts us, "Every day do something that won't compute. Love the Lord. Love the world"—and finally, "Practice resurrection."

The disciples locked in the room in John 20:19 need help in practicing resurrection. Mary has already told them that she's seen the Lord risen from the dead, but her testimony fails to penetrate their reality. Whether they don't believe her or can't imagine what her words mean, they remain prisoners of their fear and guilt.

Then Jesus is there, saying at once the most ordinary and absurd thing—"Peace be with you." Yes, it was the common greeting of the day. But "Peace be with you"? Is that a joke? Peace is the last thing that is keeping these disciples company, and the appearance of their dead teacher doesn't seem likely to improve the situation.

For Jesus, these words are neither a salutation nor an attempt at ironic humor. They are the fulfillment of a promise. The last time they were together, Jesus told his disciples that, regardless of what they were threatened with in this world, they would share in his peace. But simply saying it had not made it so. Now Jesus Christ the risen Lord has come back to make good on that promise. When he tells them "Peace be with you," not once but three times, he is giving them what they need to claim that *"shalom"* as a reality.

"Peace be with you, for death has been defeated." He shows them the holes in his hands and side, signs that his is the body that was crucified. Yet he stands before them, breathing and speaking and wearing these marks of death like a victor's medals.

"Peace be with you, for the bonds of sin are broken." He breathes his own life and his own mission into them by the power of the Holy Spirit. They will now share both his power and responsibility, offering the call to repentance and the good news that God's grace can wash away the old life and put a new one in its place.

"Peace be with you, for there is more to this world than meets the eye." He invites Thomas, and all who will come after him, to believe the truth that is too good to be true. We can break free of our demands to touch and to see and trust the witness of the apostles.

The peace Jesus offers is no anesthetic for the soul, no greeting-card platitude about the sun behind the clouds. It is the beginning of a new world, the long-awaited world of God's shalom. It comes with freedom from fear, sin, and death. Jesus opens the door that the disciples had locked; and like the mad farmer, he shows the way to resurrection reality.

In Acts we catch a glimpse of what happened after they walked through that door. The peace that Jesus promised abounds in the Jerusalem church, both in their common faith—"[They] were of one heart and soul"—and their common life—"No one claimed private ownership…but everything…was held in common" (4:32). There is no chicken and egg question: Did they share everything because "great grace was upon them" (4:33b) or did they receive great grace because "there was not a needy person among them" (4:34a)?

In the power of the Spirit, they lived what they claimed, that fear had been buried in that empty tomb at Easter. They practiced resurrection. People free from death are also free to sell off the old home place or cash in their pension if somebody else needs it. They don't have to build their security on the backs of their neighbors. Their future has been secured for them.

No wonder there was great power in their testimony to the resurrection. If they encountered those who, like Thomas, demanded proof of this miracle, they invited them home for dinner. So much for the great divide between saving souls and feeding the hungry. So much for the Bible study teacher caring for "spiritual matters" while the finance chairperson keeps an eye on "the real world." The gospel creates a new world, one in which people are no longer "afraid to know your neighbors and to die."

During my first year out of seminary, I lived in an urban Christian community that had been ministering to the homeless for over twenty years. An attorney next door was often enraged by the homeless men. For years he waged war against his neighbors, calling police, fire inspectors, the health department, and trying every bureaucratic means to shut the ministry down or push it out. But the community endured these assaults, and eventually there was a cease-fire. Relations were still tense until the day a letter arrived from this man. It contained a large check and a letter of deep regret. The neighbor asked for the community's forgiveness and closed with "Peace be with you."

There was no explanation given for this dramatic change, but I can't help thinking it was the cumulative effect of so many years spent in close proximity to one of God's outposts of peace. In his once-despised neighbors, this man came to see that the promise of reconciliation and a new beginning was not a dream. It was, instead, right next door.

Fresh Evidence

KRISTEN BARGERON GRANT

Luke 24:36b–48

"You are witnesses of these things." (Luke 24:48)

When I was in kindergarten, one of my favorite activities was "What's in the box?" The teacher cut a hand-sized hole in a box and placed a mystery object inside. You could reach in the box, smell the box, shake the box—everything but open the box. Each one of us would take a turn with the box and share what we discovered with the class. We tried to guess the right answer. "It's kind of fuzzy." "Is it a teddy bear?" "It feels like a ball, but it's pointy on the side." "Is it a football?"

We thought it was just a game, but our teacher was trying to show us how to explore the world, how to ask the right questions, put together clues, hold back wild guesses, and be patient, waiting for the right conclusion to emerge.

Jesus uses a similar pedagogy as he leads the disciples into exploring the post-Easter world. They are somewhat less eager pupils than my kindergarten class. For one thing, they are terrified. For another, they are pretty sure that they already know what they are seeing. After all, there are only two ways to explain why this man who looks like Jesus is standing before them. One is that Jesus hadn't died after all. But as much as they wanted to believe that, they knew it couldn't be true. They had seen the cross, the body, the sealed tomb. They had all the evidence they needed, and there was only one other conclusion. This was a ghost, and ghosts are not generally signs of good news.

But Jesus gently coaxes them to a third, unconsidered, incomprehensible conclusion. He doesn't explain resurrection, but instead encourages them to discover it for themselves. "Look at my hands and feet, where I was nailed to the wood. Yes, that's right. I did die. A ghost? Are you sure? Touch me. Is that what a ghost feels like? Give me some fish. Do apparitions chew and swallow? It is I. I know you don't understand it; I know you can't believe it, but go ahead. Take a guess at what God has done."

Luke tells us that the disciples "in their joy…were still disbelieving and still wondering" (24:41a). They wanted to give in to the hope that was jumping around in their bellies; they wanted to raise their hands and say, "Is it Jesus? It is; it's Jesus!" But they were so very, very afraid of getting this answer wrong. So Jesus gives them some more clues. He begins again to tell the story of God's plan to restore all of creation, from the covenant with Abraham to the exodus from Egypt, from Ezekiel's valley of dry bones to Isaiah's suffering servant. He's told them all this before, of course, but this time, in the presence of their risen Lord, the doors in the minds of the disciples are unlocked. The rejection, the suffering, the crucifixion—they weren't a detour from God's plan after all, but the final steps of God's long journey down into the plight of broken humanity. Now they are witnesses to the first steps on the other side. Not a dead man, not a ghost, but the victory of God!

And that is the role that Jesus gives to the disciples and to us in this story—we are to be witnesses. Not expert witnesses, just witnesses—people who tell the truth about what they have experienced. Throughout this Easter season, we hear some of the earliest of these testimonies: "I touched him, and he was not a ghost." "I saw the marks in his hands and feet; he was the crucified one." "We broke bread with him, and he ate." Two thousand years later, we can still give evidence of how the risen Jesus has come into our lives and retold the story of our lives in a way that opened our minds to the truth.

But those first witnesses didn't just give their testimony in words. Many of the people who saw the resurrected Jesus that day eventually offered evidence that was written in their own blood. The word translated as "witness" is *martyrs*.

Some scholars rush to point out that this meaning was a "later development," that Jesus did not intend that all his witnesses should become martyrs in the technical sense. Fair enough. But the church that grew from the blood of those martyrs knew what it was talking about. To be a Christian witness is not simply to repeat what you have heard. It is to give your whole life as evidence of the truth. Belief in the resurrected Lord can't be argued or explained *into* someone. Even Jesus didn't try that. He knew that the truth had to be seen, had to be touched, had to be experienced in his own flesh and in the living, and—if necessary—dying, witness of his disciples.

We are witnesses when we can invite someone to look into our homes, our families, our friendships, our work, our checkbooks, our day-timers—and find Jesus there. We are witnesses when we allow ourselves to be touched by folks who are lost and afraid. We are witnesses when we live in a way that defies any explanation other than the presence of the risen Christ within us. Look, touch, see, believe! It isn't a ghost. It's the living God.

Hooked on War

ANDREW WARNER

Psalm 23; John 10:11–18

"I am the good shepherd. The good shepherd lays down his life for the sheep." (John 10:11)

The navy shaped my grandfather's life. He was a retired navy officer when he died, so we held his funeral at Arlington National Cemetery. Armed guards greeted us at the gates of Fort Myer. As my family and I drove through the base, we noted the display of guns and armaments. Outside the chapel stood an honor guard.

After the family service, taps played while my grandfather's ashes were put into a horse-drawn casket and we were escorted through the cemetery—the soldiers, the horse-drawn carriage, then the family. At the burial site an American flag was folded and presented to my grandmother, and the noise of a twenty-one–gun salute made us jump.

The overwhelming power of our military and our government was on display—not just the power to defeat an enemy, but the symbolic reminder of our military's power. Even in a military funeral, we see how the military gives meaning to death, shape to destruction, and an idealistic aura to aggression.

For many years my congregation has struggled with its place and calling in a superpower nation. During the height of the cold-war confrontation with the Soviet Union, for example, we designated ourselves a "Just Peace" congregation. Without declaring ourselves pacifists, we were rejecting the military arms race and the logic of mutually assured destruction.

Now, in a different political environment, we are again grappling with the morality of American military power. Increasingly we are finding it necessary to understand how our faith affects our relationship to America, how our love of Jesus informs and even changes our love of America, and how God calls us to speak up for the powerless. Advocating for peace is requiring us to confront the seductive power of military might at a time when its allure becomes almost unbearable; dissent is seen as treason, discussion as a betrayal.

Now, in "real time" news, journalists encourage us to be embedded with the war effort. The sight of men and women from our own towns and congregations can make us instinctively support a war. The war itself is often presented with a certain glamour—"smart" bombs, quick tanks, special ops—while the media help us protect ourselves from gory reality. Chris Hedges, a former war correspondent and author of *War Is a Force Which Unites Us*, describes the seductive quality of martial power as a narcotic that can provoke in whole societies a self-righteous delirium.

Making sense of our mission and ministry in this time requires that we find some way to keep our heads clear of the narcotic of war. We must cultivate an alternative power, an alternative source of meaning. Good Shepherd Sunday may be the time to recall that we derive our identity not from the prestige of our country but from the presence of our Lord.

The gospel leads us to remember to whom we belong. "I am the good shepherd. I know my own and my own know me" (Jn. 10:14). In moments of national crises, amidst the rally cry of war, we are to know that we belong to Jesus. The seductive voice of military might drowns out the call of Jesus; in countless conflicts this has occurred, and the church has become a source of sanctimonious propaganda.

Therefore, reciting Psalm 23 is both a reminder and a confession. It reminds us that Jesus is our only shepherd, the one whose voice we must heed, and that we must confess that often we listen to the call of wolves and lazy hirelings. By reciting the twenty-third Psalm we ascribe to Jesus prerogatives that the state normally takes on for itself. It is not the state but the shepherd Jesus who is to provide for our health; the shepherd Jesus who ensures our security; the shepherd Jesus who protects us and provides for us.

It is to Jesus the shepherd that our ancestors looked in faith when they experienced anxiety, turmoil, and oppression. The Heidelberg Catechism, my denomination's FAQ on Christian life, captures this in its opening question:

"What is your only comfort, in life and in death?"

"That I belong—body and soul, in life and in death—not to myself but to my faithful Savior, Jesus Christ."

In my congregation we furnish the sanctuary with a window of Jesus as the Good Shepherd, but we do not have an American flag there, because we seek our comfort in the Lord's presence and not in the Pentagon's power.

To be led by our shepherd Jesus does not mean we are naïve about the reality of wolves and thickets and lazy hirelings who might endanger the sheep. It doesn't mean we ignore the oppression of Kurdish and Shi'ite Iraqis. It doesn't mean we overlook the threat to international peace posed by a nuclear North Korea. It doesn't mean we ignore the immorality of preemptive wars. Instead, amid all the uncertainty of this life, amid all of the real and imagined dangers, our peace comes from the presence of our shepherd Jesus, who "prepare[s] a table before me / in the presence of my enemies."

It is by remembering that Jesus is my Good Shepherd that we can find the presence of mind to speak and witness and preach in a nation overtaken by the rhetoric and the narcotic of war.

Kingdom Come

ANDREW WARNER

Psalm 22; John 15:1–8

> *For dominion belongs to the LORD,*
> *and he rules over the nations. (Psalm 22:28)*

A strange king is likely to have a strange kingdom, and the kingdom of Jesus is no exception. One glimpse of Jesus' kingdom reveals a crazy diversity of peoples feasting, worshiping, and struggling together.

Jesus gave a more nuanced image of the kingdom during his farewell conversation with the disciples. "I am the vine, you are the branches" (Jn. 15:5a). Now we see an image of a multilateral community, one in which each member is interwoven with the other. Within this community there is much "abiding"; Jesus abides in the disciples, and the disciples abide in him. There is also a constant "pruning" by God to pare away those traits and qualities that interfere with kingdom building, and to strengthen traits that ensure the health of the community. The result, perhaps, is a sense that the kingdom of Christ is marked by a deep mutual love and an ongoing push to ever greater love.

An analogous image of the kingdom comes to us in Psalm 22, where we hear that "dominion belongs to the LORD, / and he rules over the nations." That rule becomes explicit in verses that speak of the poor eating until they are satisfied, and even the dead joining in the celebration. John Calvin included the less historically accurate but morally compelling line, "All the fat ones of the earth shall eat and worship." These fat ones will not eat, however, until after the poor ones are satisfied, a direct inversion of our world today. This kingdom of God is a strange place.

Calvin also said, "Now if God, under the law, joined the full with the hungry, the noble with the mean, the happy with the wretched, much more ought this to take place at the present day under the gospel." We might make the same observation about the vineyard image: since God seeks a multilateral community of mutual love, we ought to live this way in our present day.

The difficulty is not in the image of community; nearly everyone will embrace the idea of a peaceful community. The stumbling point is not the sweetness of abiding together. Our trouble comes with the necessity of confronting those situations in which community is broken, or worse, in which human beings are attacking other human beings. What are the international implications of these readings?

In our global village, America is at war. An international debate about how one can create a more peaceful world among diverse peoples is raging. America went to war claiming that Saddam Hussein's government posed a threat to Iraq's neighbors, to the Iraqis themselves, and to America. There was evidence that Saddam used chemical and biological weapons, and exiles told disturbing stories of their treatment in Iraqi prisons. What remained uncertain was how to deal with Saddam.

In *Of Paradise and Power,* Robert Kagan imagines America and Europe tracing out two lines of Enlightenment thought. The Americans have responded with a call to war, assuming that the world is Hobbesian: nasty and brutish, with international law short-lived. This approach assumes that cultivating a more peaceful world requires the exercise of power, especially military power. Meanwhile, the Europeans have taken a Kantian approach: international peace depends on moving beyond power politics to the rule of law, negotiated change and, above all, cooperation. The church, too, wonders which of these approaches—the

Hobbesian or the Kantian, the Pentagon powers or the Turtle Bay processes—will best nourish the international community.

My congregation has lambasted the American use of military power to establish peace. They ask how any child of God could be called a "target of opportunity," and they hear the cries of those who are "collateral damage." Our reading of the gospel suggests that Jesus abides with the scared residents of Baghdad as much as he does with the soldiers invading the city.

Yet the European answer seems equally suspect. Too often the insistence on the rule of law, negotiation, and cooperation has failed to deal with horrible crimes, especially genocide. Too often abhorring military power leads to ignoring the powerless, as it did in Rwanda. Bosnia and Kosovo were saved not by negotiation but by an exercise of military power that ended genocidal campaigns. There are times when compassion might demand military action.

Jesus holds up the image of a kingdom where life is marked by a mutual love, a deep abiding with the other, and a constant struggle to ever greater care. I cannot see this vision without praying, "Thy kingdom come!" I know, like Calvin, that what God ordained ought to be here on earth: the thin ones and the fat ones feasting together. And this gives me a vision of our world as a multilateral international community where famine in Africa, genocide in Europe, and oppression in Asia are deeply felt in America because we abide in each other.

While the vision of the kingdom of God may be simple, there are no simple ways to achieve it or even make our world more like it. A military intervention in Rwanda might have stopped the killing of a million people in a hundred days. A military intervention in North Korea might hasten the killing of millions. Our task is to choose prayerfully and carefully that we might cultivate the kingdom, and not delay its arrival.

Labors of Love

LAWRENCE WOOD

John 15:9–17; 1 John 5:1–6

For the love of God is this, that we obey his commandments.
And his commandments are not burdensome. (1 John 5:3)

These are some of the nicest, happiest verses in scripture, easy to read because we all agree that we should love one another. Sunday school teachers affirm the thought; countless potholders and pillows are embroidered with it. Jeffrey Moses, in a book called *Oneness,* offers Jewish, Christian, and Buddhist texts in the hope of showing that the three religions share the message: Love one another.

Then there's Robbie. Robbie wore out her welcome at the social service agencies a long time ago. Her poverty is real—I've seen the place where she lives. But she lives a hard life and runs through help like water. After a while you want to tell her enough's enough.

Recently she called the church repeatedly to ask for groceries. When I picked up the last call, I invited her to come to the food pantry on Monday. She said she didn't have a car. Couldn't someone drive some food out her way? "I haven't had nothing to eat in four days," she moaned. Folks who come to the pantry take whatever we have, but Robbie wanted smoked turkey, lean roast beef, and a pound of coffee (decaf).

A bad storm had dumped a foot of snow on the community. Unwilling to saddle someone else with this request, I trudged down to the food pantry, filled a few grocery sacks and drove twenty miles out to her place, now and then muttering under my breath. The apartment was as awful as you can imagine: a single-story cinderblock building with a rotted roof. No one had bothered to plow the lot.

Robbie could see me coming. She stepped out of her door, smoking a cigarette. "Did you bring me the coffee?" she asked. "Decaf?"

I stopped about twenty yards out from her door. The snow was thick.

"Pastor," she said, "could you pull up a little closer?"

"Robbie, just stay there," I said, and waded through the drifts with first one sack, then the other, feeling the burden in my lower back.

She beamed, but before a conversation could begin I said, "Well, I think that's about it," and left without asking anything about her or what more she might need. It was not one of my better days in ministry.

I did, however, feel lighter. In spite of myself, I felt glad to have been of some help. And about a hundred yards down the road, I had the odd feeling that when I am judged, it will be by what I do for Robbie.

Love one another. Today's scriptures don't just advise us; they command us, with the same force that Moses brought the law down from Sinai. Jesus himself says, "I am giving you these commands so that you may love one another" (Jn. 15:17). He calls us to love whether or not we feel love. Sometimes the feeling comes first, and the work is easy. In any event, says the first letter of John, "His commandments are not burdensome."

We read these words, as we are meant to, in the context of Easter. God has given the ultimate love gift, one that recognizes and answers all the pain in the world, and it's not a warm, fuzzy feeling. For God to bring good out of all things—even out of the cross—is an act of love.

Of all the gospel writers, John gives us the most pointed post-Easter story, one in which Jesus repeatedly asks Peter, "Do you love me?" and commands him to "feed my sheep." It's a story that recognizes that even the miracle of Easter doesn't always motivate us as it ought, at least not on schedule. One by one, we come around and "we love because he first loved us" (1 Jn. 4:19), by which John means that we act. Surely God's hope is that our feeling will join our actions so that ministry happens spontaneously, naturally, and joyfully.

Today's mail brought a package from a friend in Chicago. Sam is a large, shambling, shy man who can't quite look you in the eye when he speaks, but who does the most extraordinarily kind things. He has always lived simply so he can devote most of his time to these quiet works. Whenever he baked communion bread for his church, he would bring extra loaves to those of us at the seminary. And he'd add insights from his devotional readings of Henry David Thoreau, W. H. Auden, and Wendell Berry. When I was in seminary, I was often in real need. That bread made a one-course meal for me on many Saturdays and Sundays, when hardly anybody else knew that I was desperately hungry. I didn't have a car, and I burned a lot of calories walking. Sam did without a car, too, and the unassuming, almost angelic way he ordered his life taught me a lot about ministry.

Sam is in bad health these days and shuffles around on numbed feet. Traveling by elevated train has become difficult. But getting out to do things for others "is what really gives me pleasure these days," he says. Now he'd sent me a book and a long note. At the bottom of the note was this verse: "A new heart I will give you and a new spirit I will put within you."

That is what Easter is supposed to do.

Christ's commandments are not burdensome. "My yoke is easy, and my burden is light" (Mt. 11:30). Love is the lightest of responsibilities. What else do we mean by a labor of love? The difficulty is when we take up the labor before the love. When we get it right, the work of love is hardly work at all.

Above and Beyond

LAWRENCE WOOD

Luke 24:44–53; Acts 1:1–11

While he was blessing them, he withdrew from them and was carried up into heaven. (Luke 24:51)

Just like that, Jesus is gone. He reappears just long enough to say goodbye. Like a wraith, like a dream, he leaves behind no children, no estate, no writings, no trace of himself except this feeling that his presence was real, that his absence is temporary. Christians have this uncanny feeling that he was just here. He must have just stepped out.

It's a feeling of mixed joy and grief, of doubt and near certainty. The ascension marks the moment when we pass from Jesus' time into our own.

The stories say that he is taken up into heaven—like Elijah— and while we puzzle over the physics of how this happened, we have no trouble understanding it emotionally. We know too much about loss. Loved ones are suddenly taken from us, and the manner in which they go fills us with awe. It is an amazing, dreadful thing. Even though we know that they are going to "a better place," we cannot follow and have a hard time imagining that we ever will. In the strange days afterward, we have to reconcile feeling bereft with receiving an inheritance.

So the stories about Jesus' ascension are about a Christian attitude toward death. Take away the fantastic circumstances, and here is the hard reality: Jesus is gone. He rose not just from the dead, but right up and out of our world.

Yet we cannot take away the miraculous. Indeed, the miracle is the whole point: this ascension, a second Easter, confirms that he is going to heaven. His Jewish disciples see with their own eyes that he is not going to Sheol, the realm below, but to the abode of God. He is alive, so maybe their loved ones are alive; maybe death is not the end of us. As they stand on the earth, the disciples surely can think of others who were just here and might be back soon for those they love.

Luke tells two stories about the ascension. In the first, he says that Jesus walked with the disciples "as far as Bethany," where his friends Mary and Martha lived. According to the gospel of John, Bethany was also where he raised Lazarus from the dead. So it was a significant place for him—a good place for him to spend his last moments on earth.

Let's read between the lines and imagine that he chose the place of his departure because he wanted to see Mary and Martha one last time. Perhaps they ran to meet him, threw their arms round him, shouted in amazement. Mary probably had no more tears to wet his feet. Perhaps he sat at their table and let Martha wait on him again. All the while, the wondering disciples who had traveled the few miles from Jerusalem saw why he had risen, why he had come back here. Read this way, the gospel version of the ascension is a love story.

Luke's second account of a departure site is in Acts. Here he doesn't mention Bethany, but says that Jesus ordered the disciples "not to leave Jerusalem" (Acts 1:4) for Galilee right away, instructions that are different from those in other gospels. At any rate, this version recalls the ascension of Elijah, and then surpasses it completely.

As Elijah waited for the whirlwind that would take him to heaven, his disciple Elisha asked for "a double share of [his] spirit" (2 Kings 2:9c). Sure enough, when Elisha picked up Elijah's mantle, that's what he got—a powerful dose of the Spirit. In similar fashion, Jesus promised his disciples that he would not leave them comfortless, but would give them the Spirit. He meant for them to have an inheritance. And when, in a manner of speaking, they picked up his mantle, that's what they got—a double portion. The Spirit at Pentecost! We can still feel the force of it, whistling around our ears.

This, too, is a love story. A story of how love survives loss. We are not comfortless. We don't worry too much about his absence, in part because his Spirit is so alive and present. He may have risen, but in another sense he remains on the ground. He has become his disciples. They have become him.

Carl VandeGiessen, in his horn-rimmed spectacles and red tennis shoes, remains vivid in my mind. Ten years ago he lost his wife, Ruth, after her long battle with Alzheimer's. Carl had sat at her bedside every day, even in the long years when she hadn't known him. "This is what I took my wedding vows for," he would tell me.

They had met in the Epworth League of the old Methodist Church, raised beagles together, traveled together, and maintained the romance of their marriage. When she died during Holy Week, it seemed to unnerve his only daughter. I meant to console him when I said, "Carl, I'm sorry. It's especially hard to lose her this time of year."

"Are you kidding?" he said. "This is the best time for my Ruthie. She's with God now. That's what this week is all about."

Now even Carl has gone—walking confidently in his red shoes to a realm I can only imagine.

Even as the ascension leaves us here, in the modern world, ascension points beyond it. We know little about heaven—not even, really, if it is up there—but we have a lot of hope for our loved ones. We expect to see generations and generations of them, somewhere, in a time that is neither ancient nor modern. Before we were even born, Jesus changed the way we think about the dead. I would like to see Carl again someday, but this world is not the place to seek him, because he is not here. He is risen.

Coming into Focus

BILL O'BRIEN

John 15:26–27; 16:4b–15; Acts 2:1–21

All of them were filled with the Holy Spirit and began to speak in other languages, as the Spirit gave them ability. (Acts 2:4)

"When the Advocate comes!" What was Jesus trying to tell us? His words came after an embarrassing incident. When none of us disciples was willing to wash someone else's feet, Jesus did it. Our rabbi and leader. Not until much later would we understand what he was doing, but on that night we could only listen and try to make sense of his words.

Jesus laid some heavy stuff on us, stuff about loving one another. He talked of radical things, like being hated—and hinted at the possibility of even being thrown out of synagogues. Yet he also intimated that someone—this Advocate guy—would come soon.

He had held back from talking like this on previous occasions, but we could sense that tonight we were on to something big. We argued among ourselves as to which of us would be the executive assistants. In fact, two of the brothers had a plan big enough for three—the two of them and Jesus in the middle.

Jesus ended the meal and dialogue with an intense prayer. Then he went out into the night, and everything came unraveled.

We were suddenly alone, and felt afraid and forsaken. Jesus was to have been the conquering messiah with an "In your face, Rome" attitude. What went wrong? More important, where would we go now? Who among us would claim to be a follower of a misguided memory?

Then faithful women brought the electrifying news: He is alive! From that moment on we felt as if we were on fast-forward. Jesus appeared, and met with us several times. Now he was even more focused about what was going to happen and pointed out that everything said about him in the law of Moses, the prophets, and the psalms had been fulfilled. He had suffered and risen from the dead. Now forgiveness of sins would be proclaimed to every ethnic group, starting in Jerusalem.

Again he said, "The Advocate is coming," but this time he added, "Stay in the city until you have been empowered." He was gone, and once again we didn't know what he meant. But this time it was different. This time we waited.

To the very end the disciples viewed Jesus through the paradigm that had shaped them. One reason for their misperceptions of Jesus and his kingdom priorities might be that "the ministry of the Spirit was inseparable from Jesus' physical presence with them. The disciples were so satisfied with the tangible association that none of them had asked where he was eventually going," says William E. Hull, professor at Samford University in Birmingham, Alabama.

So what difference did it make that they waited?

Pentecost gave them a new lens with which to view the Master's grand design. Gone was the competitive spirit. Gone were the visions of a conquering conquistador. Gone was any advantage of privilege. It was meltdown time, and no one was prepared for the outcome. Galileans, who were not known for multilingual skills, were suddenly proclaiming the good news in languages known only to foreigners. When the crowds needed an explanation, Simon Peter emerged as a powerful apologist and convincing proclaimer.

But except for Peter this cast had no stars—just simple Galileans empowered through the indwelling Spirit of Christ. Whether they were unnamed believers or public proclaimers, they all began a journey that would be full of surprises. As Hull says, "Ultimate reality was not to be sought in a set of timeless facts which may be mastered at any moment, but in companionship with the Spirit of truth who leads one on a pilgrimage of discovery."

And so it is today. As my own pilgrimage of discovery continues to unfold, I find my life filled with surprises. I thrill to sermons by gifted proclaimers such as Barbara Brown Taylor, Fred Craddock, and Gardner Taylor. I'm also inspired by less-known Christ followers who serve in the trenches.

In Lesslie Newbigin's Bible studies for the 1986 synod of the Church of South India, he said: "Words without deeds are empty, but deeds without words are dumb." In the mission of Jesus, said Newbigin, there is both the presence of the kingdom and its proclamation. Like a seamless robe, word and deed proclaim and authenticate the news that the kingdom is at hand. The promised Advocate is the one who makes the proper application to both persons and systems.

I once followed a team of American doctors in Venezuela. When their medical equipment did not arrive, they were forced to "make do." They partnered with local doctors and pastors and were empowered to function effectively, even miraculously in some cases—and they were changed by the experience.

I've followed an educational team to Monrovia, Liberia, where team members equipped trainers of teachers nationwide. In a war-torn climate, they brought hope to teachers who are short on resources but strong on love for the students. Hope was born anew.

In an inner-city multicultural, multiethnic church in my town, pastor and people demonstrate the will to advocate for church members, half of whom are homeless. These advocates dare to go up against the structures that not only oppress their people but also make them "invisible."

The body of Christ receives and shares the same gift that the disciples received. This gift of the Spirit is as fresh today as it was at Pentecost. That is a promise, and it still holds for those who are on a pilgrimage of discovery.

Wind Blown

BILL O'BRIEN

John 3:1–17; Romans 8:12–17

For all who are led by the Spirit of God are children of God.
For you did not receive a spirit of slavery to fall back into fear,
but you have received a spirit of adoption. When we cry,
"Abba! Father!" (Romans 8:14–15)

"The Spirit of the triune God is and will always be the life
force of the world and all that is good and hopeful in it, which
includes the hunger for God." (JOANNA ADAMS)

During an attempted coup in Indonesia in 1965, an estimated 500,000 people were killed. What did not make the headlines was the quiet revolution that began to move into a collapsed intellectual and moral vacuum. The wind of the Spirit blew fresh breezes across a wounded land and people. There was no ballyhoo or promotion by the churches. There was simply the response of untold numbers who found in the churches a haven. Forgiveness and love became the "wine and bread" of acceptance and redemption. Slaves of fear no more. Thousands were able to eucharistically sing, "Abba, Father."

I have seen the wind blowing in other places. In Ghana the statue of President Kwame Nkruma in downtown Accra was smashed. The inscription below his figure read, "Seek ye first the political kingdom." The wind of the Spirit was dealing with those who usurp power. Slaves of confusion no more. Thousands would know the real "Abba, Father."

In this country the "Jesus movement" was shaking foundations across denominational lines. I visited a church in California where those dressed in business suits sat next to barefooted hippies. Latinos, African-Americans, and whites focused on transcendent issues. Across America crowds packed stadiums in Jesus rallies. Slaves of prejudice no more. Thousands celebrated the love of "Abba, Father."

In South America, base communities sprang up. An Argentinean Pentecostal explained that Catholic base communities gather without trained leadership, focus on issues of injustice, then read the Bible to see how God would lead them. Pentecostals, by contrast, start by reading the Bible, isolate the issues that are alienating them, then seek God's leadership for solutions. Essentially, both groups come out at the same place. Methodology is not the issue when the Spirit is blowing fresh breezes across the lines that separate brothers and sisters in Christ. Slaves of denominational pride no more. Thousands could recognize an inclusive "Abba, Father."

The wind of the Spirit blew open prison doors. Nelson Mandela walked into freedom with responsibility. I was mesmerized when I saw him appear on the balcony of a building in Cape Town, face an awed audience of half a million, and acknowledge the reality of the past. Then he said, "The rest of my life I place in your hands." It was a commitment of trust and solidarity. Slaves of apartheid no more. Thousands could celebrate a merciful "Abba, Father."

The wind is blowing. God is at work through the church and beyond the church. Political systems resist anything beyond themselves and the elite class they serve while at the same time the country's churches may be poor, weak, and helpless. But Jesus demonstrated that there is always room for surprises. Mangers, refugee situations, nonchic neighborhoods—these seem to be fertile ground for a new gust of the Spirit. Should it be a surprise then that the dynamic churches of the world are now in the

Southern Hemisphere and the East? The ecclesiological tectonic plates have shifted! Is this the first time for such a major turn?

In the first century a shift occurred when Gentiles were accepted as equally legitimate members of the body of Christ. Trauma and pain came to Paul and other advocates who pioneered such innovation. But these paradigm-tinkerers stood their ground and ultimately became the predominant voice in the church.

Again the wind shifted, moving out of the Mediterranean and going west. In theological debates hammered out during the fourth and fifth centuries, Berbers and Teutonics shaped doctrines that became the legacy of Western Christendom.

Centuries later the third shift is in full swing. Why did the Spirit wait so long? Wouldn't every 500 years be a decent interval, like the time frame for a super jubilee? Predicting God's ways, however, is a futile effort. Cause and effect, predictability and measurement collapse in the face of the mighty wind of a purposeful Spirit.

There is a downside to a shift. Those who inhabit the landscape of the last shift often do not know that things have changed. It's not that they don't agree with what the Spirit is doing, it's that they don't see it! They don't see the untold millions from areas marked as "mission fields" who are rising up to cry, "Abba, Father" and sharing, as co-heirs with Christ, in his sufferings. In Africa and Asia, they bear ridicule, harassment, and even death as a mark of belonging to a community of faith.

Many people are motivated to live out the good news cross-culturally. The category of "missionary" is no longer broad enough to include all of these Christians. Instead, global migration shapes new categories, as one member of a family travels abroad to provide income for family back home, or someone transfers into a different country at the request of a business. Students are in flux. If led by the Spirit of God, all of these people bear witness as they go.

No church or movement can claim ownership of the Spirit, which is interactive with the Father and the Son in the overall *missio Dei*. As at Pentecost, the Spirit came as defender of Jesus and a faithful teacher about the things of God. Are we truly on the threshold of a new apostolic era? If so, what church will want to miss it?

The Greatest of All Shrubs

WILLIAM H. WILLIMON

Mark 4:26–34

Sometimes Jesus tells us stories in order to encourage us. What better time for encouragement than now as the church limps into the summer doldrums? What better way to encourage us than with parables of seeds? Take a tiny seed, allow it to lie secretly in the ground. Surprise! The little seed sprouts and a rich harvest occurs. Yet here in early summer, a more realistic parable would speak of shrinking garments, raisins in the sun, and my withered shrubbery in drought-stricken Durham.

"With what can we compare the kingdom of God, or what parable shall we use for it?" (Mk. 4:30) asks Jesus. He answers with a parable. Take a tiny, very tiny, mustard seed. Plant it, let it lie secretly in the ground. It germinates and over time that seed will sprout and become a glorious shrub. A shrub? "Yeah," says Jesus. "A shrub. It gets to be maybe four or five feet high, even. A shrub so tall that even birds can perch on its branches." Small birds, I dare say. "All right, small birds. Still, quite impressive," says Jesus. "With many such parables he spoke the word to them, as they were able to hear it" (Mk. 4:33).

When triumphalist Luke tells this parable later, he has Jesus say that the seed "grew and became a tree" (Lk. 13:19). Matthew, wanting to be both Markan realistic and Lukan optimistic, has Jesus say, "It is the greatest of shrubs and becomes a tree" (Mt. 13:32). I suppose we are to be impressed that this "smallest of all the seeds on earth" (Mk. 4:31b) has produced a shrub. Nevertheless, a shrub is still a shrub, however Mark measures it.

However, if you are a pastor you have to love Mark for leaving the mustard shrub as a shrub. You have to admire Mark for letting Jesus hook us with this great buildup about the miracle of seeds growing only to end with nothing more to show for it than a shrub. When Jesus asks, "With what can we compare the kingdom of God?" and then answers by calling the kingdom a shrub, you know that Jesus is not only having a good time with us but also trying to show us something about the kingdom that is not easy to see.

My colleague Dan Via has argued that the theme of concealment that runs throughout Mark's gospel, the alleged "messianic secret," is a paradox. Sometimes Jesus appears concealed so that he might be revealed. The purpose of the concealment is so that Jesus might be revealed in all of his mysterious ambiguity. Via believes that a central mode of Mark's presentation of the gospel is irony. Mark's Jesus appears to us as paradoxical, mysterious, concealed, not because Jesus has a stake in secrecy, but because to our inadequate perception what is real (the kingdom of God) will inevitably seem at first hidden and mysterious.

For all the miraculous gains made by this kingdom and its Lord, the results remain unimpressive. So we look at the opening round of Jesus' assault upon the world and ask, "Are you the one who is to come, or are we to wait for another?" (Mt. 11:3; Lk. 7:20). Even after he tells us that his is a narrow way, we look around at our little band after Easter and ask, "Lord, is this the time when you will restore the kingdom to Israel?" (Acts 1:6). Little wonder that, already by the time of the earliest gospel, we are tiring of sowing tiny seeds and are ready for some significant harvest. So Jesus tells us this story of the little mustard seed that grew into this great big bush.

Here is a story told not only for the church's encouragement, but also for our rebuke. It invites us to challenge the person who criticizes Teresa of Calcutta because she appears to be less interested in structural social change (power politics) than in one-to-one acts of charity with the dying. The story rebukes the person who refuses to give up a Saturday to work on the Habitat for Humanity house because "we ought to be changing housing laws rather than building houses for the poor one at a time." Such responses testify to the hypocrisy of our posturing about structural, political, and social change that costs us nothing personally. We have convinced ourselves that if anything significant were being done by God, it would be something big.

Jesus wants us to think small. Tiny seeds. Unimpressive shrubs. Perhaps Jesus would be impressed by the evangelist who sleeps at the White House or the bishop who rebukes the president. But this parable suggests that Jesus might be even more impressed by the pastor in North Dakota who has never even seen the White House, much less talked to the president, because he has been serving the eucharist for the past thirty years to a hundred souls in a little church at a remote crossroads.

The church is impaired, the kingdom is endangered, but not by the world's continuing criticism of it as ineffective and insignificant. The church is endangered when we are tempted to derive our status from those forms of power and significance valued by the world. I have heard United Methodist bishops refer to themselves as CEOs. My own United Methodist Book of Discipline reads more like a personnel manual for IBM than a handbook of church discipline for a people called to be the world's light and salt.

To some this may seem like making a theological virtue out of a sociological necessity. We mainliners are losing numbers so fast that we had better glorify our coming minority status as a sign of fidelity. "We never wanted to be a tree anyway." The parable suggests that fidelity is first a gift of God rather than the result of the church trying to be this or that. That being said, the North American church might come to see its present situation as a providential gift enabling it to recover the church's minority status as intrinsic to its mission. History teaches us that, the world being what it is, whenever the church is faithful, the world has always characterized it as small and therefore insignificant.

Our encouragement is the parable's proclamation that, though beginnings seem small and though results appear insignificant, there will be a harvest. The Lord of the harvest gives growth, though not always the growth we expect, and there will be harvest, though not always at the times or in the mode for which we plan.

Sail On

BILL O'BRIEN

Mark 4:35–41; 2 Corinthians 6:1–13

> *And they were filled with great awe and said to one another, "Who then is this, that even the wind and the sea obey him?" (Mark 4:41)*

Evening came at last. All day Jesus had taught the large crowds, using parables as bridges to minds and hearts. His pulpit was a boat, providing a way to connect with the throngs without getting crushed. But as darkness was about to overtake the light, he told the disciples he wanted to go to the other side of the lake. "Leaving the crowd behind, they took him with them in the boat, just as he was" (Mk. 4:36).

Just as he was. Is there anything more draining than constantly giving oneself intellectually, emotionally, physically, and spiritually to a demanding public, day in and day out? To the stern of the boat he went, just as he was, and fell into a deep sleep.

It must have been the mother of all squalls. Some of the disciples were seasoned fishermen, skilled in the art of navigating dangerous waters. But this was a red alert. They were going to perish—and the one person who might turn the situation around was sleeping peacefully in the boat's place of honor, the stern. They woke Jesus up with a strident "Don't you care, Teacher?" But he did not respond to their lack of faith. Instead he responded to the peace within himself and produced a calm that impacted nature as well as the frightened disciples. The disciples were amazed. "Who is this? Even the winds and waves obey him."

A couple of decades later the apostle Paul had many experiences that threatened his life. Where was Jesus when Paul needed him? He was shipwrecked three times, and spent a night and a day adrift on the open sea. Five times Jews applied thirty-nine lashes to his back. He was beaten with a rod, stoned, and spent many nights in jail cells, sleepless and hungry.

Wake up, Master. Don't you care? Was the miraculous rescue from the forces of nature limited to the days when Jesus was present on earth? Is God really sovereign over the cosmos, including the earth and all its elements? If so, why doesn't God stop wars? Why do children suffer from cancer? Why does hostility invade homes and splinter relationships? Why do boundaries of exclusiveness divide us over race, color, and creed?

Paul's life was determined not by boundaries, but by the center. He placed the One who was the center of his life in the honored place—the stern of the heart. Paul knew that the God of Abraham, Isaac, and Jacob, the God and Father of our Lord Jesus Christ, neither slumbers nor sleeps. It was not delivery from life's dangers that defined a miracle; it was the coping power, the power present in any life situation, that bore witness to the mighty power and presence of God.

To the Corinthian Christ-followers Paul showed himself to be a servant of God: in troubles, hardships, and distresses; in beatings, imprisonment, and riots. In patience and kindness he remained genuine, yet was regarded as an imposter. He knew how to rejoice though sorrowful; how to be poor yet make many rich; how to have nothing yet possess everything. From the heart Paul learned the true meaning of freedom, and he modeled it.

Through many dangers, toils, and snares he had already come. So Paul could say to followers of the way, "Do not worry about anything, but in everything by prayer and supplication with thanksgiving let your requests be made known to God. And the peace of God, which surpasses all understanding, will guard your hearts and your minds in Christ Jesus" (Phil. 4:6–7).

The experience the disciples had with Jesus on the Sea of Galilee preceded the cross, the resurrection, and Pentecost. No wonder they asked themselves who this man was, this man who could rebuke the wind. The wonder of the miracle took precedence over the man.

But Paul could say he wanted to know Christ and the power of his resurrection and the fellowship of sharing in his sufferings. That is why, in spite of the pain of prior experiences, he could forget what was behind and strain toward what was ahead. Paul's centered life pressed toward the goal to win the prize for which God called him heavenward in Christ Jesus.

A few years ago my wife and I faced what was our "mother of all squalls" experience. Without warning, a brain attack took away use of the right side of her body.

My initial response was, "God, we are drowning—don't you care?"

Early one morning I read Psalm 84. In that psalm of ascent two of the verses jumped off the page: "Blessed are those whose strength is in you, / who have set their hearts on pilgrimage. / As they pass through the Valley of Baca, / they make it a place of springs" (vv. 5–6a, NIV). A peace began to settle in even before we would know what the outcome was to be. The miracle of God's presence, accompanied by the power to live in any situation, was all we needed. I took a pen in hand and wrote the following:

> How blessed are those whose hearts are set on pilgrimage
> Who wait upon the Lord in a dry land.
> The shepherd hears their cry and gently opens
> Springs of living water right where they stand.
> Now with a new song they lift up their voices,
> To their great God a hymn of praise is due.
> The Christ of Calvary's victory stands before them
> And bids them follow through his grave to life anew.

When Christ is invited into the stern of the heart, the miracle of presence and power equip us for any eventuality.

Begging to Give

BILL O'BRIEN

2 Corinthians 8:7–15

For if the eagerness is there, the gift is acceptable according to what one has—not according to what one does not have. (2 Corinthians 8:12)

"The past is not over," said Odessa Woolfolk of the Birmingham Civil Rights Institute. Speaking to my divinity school class, Woolfolk spoke of systems that continue to oppress and seriously limit access to resources that are basic to any human being. With slavery a thing of the past, with segregation banned, with the right to vote for everyone, what is the problem? It is access.

All families need access to adequate housing, a healthy diet, good education, and security. But for huge numbers of people, those kinds of needs are fantasy. Over a billion persons live on less than one dollar a day, and many get far less than that. Simple shelter, clean drinking water, and basic health care are not a part of their lives.

The paralyzing effect of affluence takes its toll on middle- and upper-class people. Multiple choices in housing, food, education, and entertainment blind many of us to the "invisible" communities—at home and abroad. When those communities do make it onto radar screens, we often blame the needy for their own problems. Some of us say we must quit throwing money away in foreign aid or domestic welfare. In the U.S., the government turns a friendly face to faith communities and asks them to meet the overwhelming needs of the poor, the homeless, and the dispossessed.

I love the story of the churches in Macedonia. Paul refers to Macedonian Christians, or the province, sixteen times in six of his letters. Three of his letters were to churches in Macedonia, a prosperous region. The Via Egnatia was a major east-west route that ran through it. Although the province enjoyed economic advantage, Christians in Macedonia were extremely poor and had experienced some kind of severe trial. Yet when faced with the opportunity to help the beleaguered church in Jerusalem, their response was magnanimous.

Paul wrote to the church in Corinth, reminding its members of the offering they had begun collecting a year earlier for the Jerusalem church. He had bragged about them to the Macedonian believers, and now he asked them to hurry up and complete their part of the offering. Paul wanted the Corinthians to know about the grace that God had given to the Macedonian churches, about how their overflowing joy and extreme poverty had welled up in rich generosity. They begged for the opportunity to share in this service to the Jerusalem Christians, and then wound up giving beyond their ability.

The secret to that kind of attitude lay in their commitment to the Lord first, then to their leaders, including Paul. Somewhere early in the discipleship process, they must have been taught that the earth is the Lord's and everything in it. They owned nothing. They were ambassadors of another kingdom; therefore, they were stewards of all that passed through their hands.

I imagine Paul taught the Macedonian believers the same thing he shared with the Ephesians. "Do something useful with your hands, that you may have something to share with those in need" (Eph. 4:28). Evangelist Tom Skinner, author of *Black and Free,* believed it was a duty to teach the poor church to give from the very outset. Poverty does not negate the role of stewardship. Skinner said that if a church assumes a "poor me" attitude and is only on the receiving end, it will not start giving even when it is more able to do so. Clearly, Macedonia was a model to those more able to give.

Even as Paul compared the earnestness of the Corinthians with that of the Macedonians, he ultimately was comparing their love with that of the Master. He reminded them of the grace of the Lord Jesus Christ, that though he was rich, yet for their sakes he became poor, so that they through his poverty might become rich.

Paul explained to the Philippian church that all believers should have the same attitude as that of Christ, who, being in very nature God, did not consider equality something to be grasped, but made himself nothing, taking the very nature of a servant. He was exalted through obedience—even obedience to death. (See Phil. 2.)

Today I marvel at churches in Latin America, Africa, and Asia that are twenty-first–century Macedonias. A few years ago I was with a group in Nanjing, China, for a dialogue with leaders of the China Christian Council. On Sunday we visited various churches in the city. An older Chinese woman now living in Los Angeles chose to visit a church across the river from Nanjing, a poor church composed of farmers. The nine hundred who were present for the service wanted to hear a word from their sister from the states, so Mrs. Chang brought greetings from her church in Los Angeles. She told how the Lord had added many to their church and how they were currently building a large new addition. Then after a word of blessing for this church, she took her seat. At the close of the worship time, Mrs. Chang was called back to the front. The pastor said her words had thrilled their hearts. They wanted her to have the morning offering to help with the new building in Los Angeles—about $140. When their overflowing joy welled up in generosity, they gave beyond their ability.

One might say that the American church did not need that money. They were not in the position of the Jerusalem church that was languishing. But they did need the reminder not to lose sight of the real need of people, either in L.A. or in China, for the past is not over.

The answer just might lie in churches that are begging—begging for the privilege of standing with those in need and applying a holistic gospel to the systems that deprive people of their dignity.

Paul Almighty

JOANNA ADAMS

Mark 6:1–13; 2 Corinthians 12:2–10

*On behalf of such a one I will boast, but on my own behalf I
will not boast, except of my weaknesses. (2 Corinthians 12:5)*

In the blockbuster movie *Bruce Almighty,* a television newsman is
given a set of divine powers, including the capacity to perform
such miracles as the parting of a bowl of tomato soup, à la Moses'
parting of the Red Sea. When God wants to communicate with
Bruce, God displays a telephone number on Bruce's pager. In the
weeks after the movie's release, anyone who shared God's seven-
digit number was besieged with calls from cranks, practical jokers,
and a lot of people desperate to connect with God.

I remember a friend telling me about her sister-in-law, who
had found such a connection in a weekly prayer group, then
became insufferable to the other members of the family. "We just
can't be spiritual enough for Evelyn," my friend sighed. My friend
stopped worrying about spiritual inadequacy, however, when she
heard that the prayer group had prayed for a set of color-
coordinated kitchen appliances for one of its members. Yes, the

appliances arrived at the member's home. But they still needed to be paid for by means of an easy-payment plan.

Long ago, a group of Jewish-Christian missionaries came to Corinth, Greece, and claimed to have a special connection, or "easy line," to God. They criticized the apostle Paul and claimed to have more spiritual power than he had ever dreamed of.

Paul had one of the more extraordinary spiritual experiences a person could imagine, being "caught up in the third heaven," but he never considered praying for such a thing; and after it happened he kept it to himself. He could have impressed people if he had told them about his spectacular trip to paradise, where he was given a revelation of "things that are not to be told, that no mortal is permitted to repeat." Heavenly journeys were all the rage in Paul's day, but his lips remained sealed for fourteen years. When he finally felt compelled to speak of his experience to his erstwhile friends in Corinth, he used the third person, as if he were speaking of someone else. Remembering Paul today, one wonders what in the world has happened to the perfectly respectable Christian value of humility. Indeed, much more than virtue is involved. The very nature of the gospel of Jesus Christ is at stake when those who claim to follow Jesus spend their energies boasting about how good they are, as opposed to the rest of us; how accessible the Almighty is to them, as opposed to the rest of us; how efficacious their prayer life is, as opposed to ours.

After Paul's unexpected ecstatic experience, something else happened that he had not expected or prayed for. A "thorn was given [him] in the flesh, a messenger of Satan to torment" him (12:7b). Why? Twice in one verse, Paul offers what is, to him, the obvious explanation: "To keep me from being too elated." If you get too carried away about yourself—if you impress yourself and want to impress others with your spiritual high-water marks—you are likely to get confused about who really has the power to save and how that power is released in the world. According to the original story, it was not so much in glorious spectacle but in suffering death. Foolishness in the eyes of the world.

So what was that dratted thorn? Oceans of ink have flowed with speculation about it. Was it a physical disability? a mental illness? a spiritual torment or a chronic temptation that Paul constantly had to wrestle to the ground but could never finally defeat? Presumably the Corinthians knew what it was, so he had no need to name it for them. Presumably every Corinthian had his or her own thorn to deal with. So do we. What does the old Joe South song say? "I beg your pardon. I never promised you a rose garden." But thorns we get. They are chronic. They cause pain.

For Paul, who wasn't one to complain much, the problem with the thorn and the reason he had asked the Lord to remove it three times was that he was worried that it might interfere with his purpose in life, which was to share the good news of Christ. No wonder he called it "a messenger of Satan"! Yet even with Paul's wish to serve, even with his good motives, the Lord did not answer his prayer as he had asked or expected. This instead was the answer: "My grace is sufficient for you, for power is made perfect in weakness" (12:9a). Good-bye, Paul Almighty. Hello, servant, through whom the power of Christ can shine. Good-bye any wish for perfection. Hello, hope for every long-suffering, imperfect, demon-fighting, disability-challenged, stage-frightened, anxiety-ridden, on-the-verge-of-a-pity-party servant of the gospel who ever lived. Don't worry about what you bring to the table. If you are called, God's grace will be sufficient for you.

Surely the sufficiency of grace was what lay behind Jesus' sending out his first twelve apostles without anything "except a staff; no bread, no bag, no money in their belts" (Mk. 6:8). When those disciples hit the road, they had nothing to show for themselves but the power of Christ. As another friend of mine has put it, isn't it his power, finally, that gets the job done?

During the Civil War, a hastily written prayer was found in the pocket of a fatally wounded soldier. "I received nothing that I asked for, but all I had hoped," it read. "My prayers were answered." Our prayers will also be answered, in God's own time and God's own way, and when they are, I hope we won't brag about it, but rather be humbly grateful and give the glory to God Almighty.

A Terrible Text

JOANNA ADAMS

Mark 6:14–29

> *Immediately the king sent a soldier of the guard with orders to bring John's head. He went and beheaded him in the prison, brought his head on a platter, and gave it to the girl. Then the girl gave it to her mother. (Mark 6:27–28)*

If preachers are ever inclined to take a break from the rigors of the lectionary, it is in the middle of the summer, when the blackberries are ripe for picking and the pews are thinly populated. I have a special place in my heart for those who bravely shape and roll out a summer set of sermons based on "Terrible Texts" or "Passages I'll Bet You Didn't Know Were in the Bible." By the time the fireflies have gone, the congregation and the preacher have struggled through the account of poor Uzzah's being struck dead for reaching out his hand to steady the ark when it wobbled on its way to Jerusalem (2 Sam. 6:6–7) or the heartbreaking saga about Jephthah's daughter, who lost her life because of her father's foolish promise (Judg. 11). These will surely make the summer hit parade.

Because the lectionary usually spares us such grim episodes, it is noteworthy that Mark's account of the beheading of John the Baptist is an assigned gospel lesson in the month of July. I confess that I have never heard nor preached a sermon on the passage, and for good reason. You can put your ear to the ground and listen as hard as you can, but you will not detect a single note of authentic joy or hope anywhere in the vicinity. What you will hear is a sordid tale of anger and revenge, resentment and death. Jesus is never even mentioned. Instead, the plot revolves around two men—John the Baptist and Herod Antipas, tetrarch of Galilee; and two women—Herodias, Herod's wife, formerly married to Herod's brother Philip, and Herod's niece/stepdaughter, also named Herodias. (Jewish historian Josephus identified her as "Salome," which helps with the confusion.)

John had gone to Herod and told the ruler that his marriage was a moral outrage. (Herod had broken up his brother's marriage to take Herodias as his wife.) Herod did not like John's words, but the blushing bride was so infuriated that she wanted to kill him. Herod, who spent most of his time trying to please people, decided to lock John the Baptist in prison.

Things came to a head, if you will pardon the expression, when Herod threw a birthday banquet for himself. The entertainment for the evening was provided by the family lotus blossom, Salome, who danced up such a storm that Herod told her that she could have anything she wanted. When Salome asked her mother what she should ask for, Herodias shot back, "The head of John the baptizer!" (Mk. 6:24b).

Salome returned to the party and made the demand, adding her own personal touch by requesting that John's head be served on a platter as the last course at the banquet. Herod did not really want to grant the request, but he couldn't afford to lose face in front of Salome or his VIP guests, who had heard him make his foolish promise. After the grotesque scene ended, what was left of John was claimed by his disciples and laid in a tomb.

Though Jesus is never mentioned, the key to understanding why this sorry saga shows up where it does in Mark's gospel is its relation both to the growing fame of Jesus and the success of his disciples. On their very first missionary journey, the disciples had "cast out many demons, and anointed with oil many who were sick and cured them" (Mk. 6:13). Just as in the opening verses of Mark the beginning of Jesus' ministry is linked to the work of John the Baptist, so here, John's death foreshadows Jesus' death. Just as John's willingness to speak the truth to power leads to his being taken prisoner and suffering a terrible death, so it will be with Jesus. Herod will become Pilate. The means of execution will be a cross rather than a sword, but the end will be the same. And so it will be for many of the early followers of Jesus, readers of Mark, who will be imprisoned and die for the sake of the gospel.

Those who follow Jesus in any age must never become carried away with the naïve notion that faithfulness to God will ever be easy. The road is rocky. Resistance is real, as is the fecklessness of many who are entrusted with political power and who are threatened by any authority other than their own. It is not that they are all bad or all good. It is that when things get tight, expediency and people-pleasing usually carry the day.

And, of course, there is the capacity for evil that can flourish in any human heart, regardless of outward beauty or grace. There is also the ferocity of wounded pride and the wish for revenge. These are too real.

Over the desk in my study is a small, framed photograph taken in the early 1930s. My grandmother Anna, a preacher's wife who died before I was born, sits in a wicker rocker, a shawl around her ample shoulders and a Bible open in her hands on her lap. Whatever is the opposite of Herodias and Salome was my grandmother. I wonder what she thought about the beheading of John the Baptist. I am sure she knew the story. And I think she also knew that it would take more than a decapitation to stop the truth of God, more than a crucifixion to stop the Son of God, more than persecution to stop the mission of God.

All the important guests at Herod's birthday party would never know what my grandmother knew—that after Herod was sealed in his grave, you and I would be thinking about John the Baptist and rejoicing that gospel power was still on the prowl.

We Were Aliens

WILLIAM H. LAMAR IV

Ephesians 2:11–22; Mark 6:30–34, 53–56

> *Remember that you were at that time without Christ, being aliens from the commonwealth of Israel, and strangers to the covenants of promise, having no hope and without God in the world. (Ephesians 2:12)*

Only 87 entries separate "America" and "amnesia" in *Merriam Webster's Collegiate Tenth Edition*. Perhaps the name of our nation and the term designating memory loss live in the same lexical neighborhood because they are so fond of each other. I like to imagine them taking road trips together, drinking cognac, smoking cigars, and reminiscing about days gone by. But the reminiscing part poses a problem. "Amnesia" is memory loss based on physical trauma or selectively ignoring events that cause discomfort; "America" is a great nation with a proclivity toward overlooking its painful past. Eureka! "America" and "amnesia" are friends of convenience. One doesn't want to reminisce, while the other is incapable of it.

Glossing over the past is as American as apple pie. Ask an American about evil, and you will hear about Saddam Hussein or Adolf Hitler. To be sure, these two men personify death, brutality, and destruction, but demonizing them does not help us. The ovens of Auschwitz stain humanity, but what about American trees bearing the strange, bloody fruit of black bodies? Hussein's genocide against non-Arabs is a travesty, but explain too, if you can, why there are so few Choctaw, Shawnee, Cherokee, and Seminoles in this land. The hatred we see in the world has lived, and still lives, in America the beautiful.

Our political leaders designate "other" people and places as evil and engage in questionable policies because they know the body politic will buy that sort of rhetoric. We want to think of ourselves as good and others as bad. Thank God for biblical theology's insistence that human beings are equally capable of love and hate, of caring for one another and of crucifying undesirables.

The writer of Ephesians is on a mission from God to remind the Ephesians of their past. He knows that if the Gentiles forget who they were, they will soon presume that God owes them something and decide to live under their own merit and not under God's grace. Salvation, the writer insists, came to the Gentiles by grace through faith, not through human works, but as a gift from God. Thus we can eliminate a reason to boast of anything but God's mercy. The warning sign is up: "Do Not Forget the Gracious Acts of God." To keep them from forgetting the writer calls on the Ephesians to remember…

> Remember that there was a time when the chosen or "circumcised" derided you and called you the "uncircumcised." Remember that you were without Christ and were strangers to the covenant, lacking hope and apart from God. And magnificently Jesus brought you from afar into the very presence of God through his blood. Jesus did not make peace between you and God; Jesus *is* the peace between you and God. He tore down the wall of separation and made one people of Jew and gentile.
>
> Remember that you could not enter the temple, the holy place. There was a barrier between you and Israel even in God's house! Jesus came and proclaimed peace; through him you have been granted access to the Father. You are aliens no more, but citizens and members of the household of God. (2:11–22, auth. trans.)

This passage must be recalled time and time again. The Ephesians needed to hear their heritage—a story of exclusion that became a story of inclusion. This message is equally important for the church in America today. The proclamations of many churches would lead you to think that Gentiles have always had equal access to God. And most of us are not taught that we are the Gentiles. The scandal of that particularity stings, that God revealed Godself to Israel and chose them—not us—as God's people. That is hard for us to swallow. And let's not jump too quickly into our acceptance through Christ. Let's stay out here for a while—alienated, locked out, cast away. The truth of our past drives us to amnesia because we want to forget that there was a time when we did not belong.

But thank God for that fact. We are the sole superpower, but we did not belong. We have the smartest bombs and the biggest guns, but we did not belong. We have the strongest economy in the world, but we did not belong. We cannot allow amnesia to seduce us into believing that we have always had access. Honest meditation on the fact that we did not belong will make us more humble as a church, a people, and a nation. We will be less likely to alienate others if we remember that we were aliens. We will be less likely to demonize the history and sinfulness of others if we remember our own troubled past. And maybe, just maybe, we will be a little more merciful and a lot more thankful for the one who is our peace with God and God's people.

In the gospel lesson, Jesus continues his work of tearing down walls and extending God's mercy to those who are scattered and alienated. He had compassion on the crowds, as he has had on us, because they were like sheep without a shepherd. He began teaching them, beckoning the lost and leaderless, the alienated and disinherited, and teaching them that God had come near. Repent and believe this good news—God is for you, God seeks you, God loves you. All people are recipients of this good news—Jews and Gentiles alike.

Remembering our past helps us to appreciate and not take for granted the mighty acts of God through Christ Jesus. We did not belong. Our relationship with God is not a right, but a gift. My prayer is that we will stop taking the gift for granted.

Chasing Jesus

WILLIAM H. LAMAR IV

Ephesians 3:14–21; John 6:1–21

A large crowd kept following him, because they saw the signs
that he was doing for the sick. (John 6:2)

When we use words, images, and pictures to communicate who
God is and what God has done, we speak of God as "shepherd,"
"mother," "fire," "cloud," and "love." We relate to God using ideas
that are common to our shared human experience because that is
all we know how to do. Thus the scripture writers speak of God
anthropomorphically, and God becomes a father with two
bewildered sons in Jesus' parable or, as God was for my grandparents, a lawyer and a doctor. Speaking of God in human terms
helps us know God.

When I came to the community where I currently serve as
pastor, I thought about God's relationship with this place. I looked
for an image that would speak to our experience in one of the
poorest communities in central Florida. We needed a face, a story,
and an identity. Slumlords rule here, drugs are rampant, low
wages are common, and streets full of litter tell of lives littered

with hopelessness. I needed a living, breathing metaphor for the community I was called to serve. I found that metaphor in John 6.

"A large crowd kept following him, because they saw the signs that he was doing for the sick." My community is the crowd following Jesus because they saw what he was doing. Why follow a healer? Because they knew that they were sick. But we must not limit the comparison to the community around Jesus long ago, or to my congregational community. You and I must see that we too are in the crowd. We too are suffering from maladies of one sort or another, and this is why we seek after Jesus. We are sick. In desperation we seek someone to heal us. When we recognize our illness, we go to great lengths to find healing.

Our culture frowns upon the desperation demonstrated by this crowd. Being desperate for material things and status and position is one thing our culture understands, and even applauds. But chasing Jesus is not likely to earn one a standing ovation. Yet the crowd's longing for Jesus reminds us of the image of the psalmist longing for God—"like a deer panting for water." Or in the songwriter's parlance, we need God "like the desert needs rain."

So when Jesus goes up the mountain, the crowd follows. He does not turn away those who seek him. All human beings know the pain of rejection, of being unwanted. In my community, doors have been shut in our faces. Windows have been locked. But Jesus sits atop the mountain waiting. Imagine the people he sees coming toward him. There are liars, thieves, and beggars. There are murderers and malcontents. But Jesus does not ask for résumés or credentials. He simply welcomes all who appear.

Then Jesus feeds them. He knows our hunger because he has experienced it himself. Did he not teach us to pray, "Give us this day our daily bread?" But even before the people ask for bread, Jesus, the Bread of Life, is making provision for them. And from where does the provision come? A quiet little boy with fish and bread shares with Jesus, and something astonishing happens. The whole crowd is blessed. No gift given to the Lord is given in a vacuum. Instead, all gifts given to God bless the entire body of Christ. We climb the hill in need of healing and receive what the body needs to be made well—adequate nourishment. But fish and bread are not all he comes to give us. He comes to give us himself; he comes to give us God. We may misinterpret his desire to bless us and try to crown him an earthly king, but his kingdom is not based on human needs or human approval. His kingdom is initiated and sustained by God.

We employ human terms to communicate who God is to one another, and God responds by employing human terms to communicate with us. But God uses not only words, pictures, and images. God also uses Jesus, the Word become flesh and dwelling among us. We look for ways to express who God is, and here God is among us in Jesus Christ, feeding, forgiving, healing, and reconciling.

This is why Paul bursts into exuberant praise in Ephesians 3. What was hidden is now revealed. Jesus Christ is among us and has granted to the hungry crowds access to God in boldness and confidence through faith. No more words and laws and oracles, but God with us, for us, and in us. So we, along with Paul, bow before God. We pray for spiritual strength. We pray that the God who has come will dwell in our hearts through faith. We pray for the power to comprehend, with the saints, the breadth and length and height and depth of God's love in Christ.

We praise God because we, as members of the crowd, have tasted the generosity of God through Christ. This love surpasses all knowledge. Love that feeds hungry crowds cannot be explained. Love that turns no one away cannot be explained. Love that causes one to sacrifice oneself for the sake of another cannot be explained. This love was experienced when a crowd scaled a mountain to receive it and when Jesus mounted a cross to "shed it abroad." When we finally acknowledge that books and lectures and sermons cannot adequately contain what we want to say about God's love and God's mercy, we explode in doxology: "Now to him who by the power at work within us is able to accomplish abundantly far more than all we can ask or imagine, to him be glory in the church and in Christ Jesus to all generations, forever and ever. Amen" (Eph. 3:20–21).

Joined at the Heart

PAUL STROBLE

Ephesians 4:1–16

> *But speaking the truth in love, we must grow up in every way into him who is the head, into Christ, from whom the whole body, joined and knit together by every ligament with which it is equipped, as each part is working properly, promotes the body's growth in building itself up in love. (Ephesians 4:15–16)*

A newspaper cartoon depicts two men tied to a post and surrounded by enemies. One says to the other, "Someday we'll look back on this and laugh." While the apostle Paul doesn't strike me as the kind of person who'd crack a joke or offer a sarcastic quip in a tight situation, he does share this ability to look positively at a crisis situation.

In the middle portion of Ephesians, Paul refers to himself as a prisoner for the Lord (chapters 3, 4, and 6). Some scholars believe Ephesians is a pseudonymous letter, but whether or not Paul actually wrote Ephesians, he did suffer in prison during his ministry, and he wrote Philemon and Philippians while in prison. In these letters we see Paul taking himself, his readers, and his congregations from despair to hope, from sorrow to joy, and from suffering to gratitude.

Buddhists have an explanation for the suffering that Paul endured. They would say that he was burdened with something he hated (prison confinement, hunger, pain, fatigue), that he desired freedom from that thing, and thus he suffered. Most of us can understand this: we can think of situations from which we couldn't immediately extricate ourselves. Some of these were relatively minor: a traffic jam, a long line, a full waiting room. Others fell under "big stuff": an illness, an unsatisfactory job (or joblessness), an overseas tour of duty, perhaps even incarceration.

One of my mother's favorite westerns features the hero and "damsel" tied to a bundle of dynamite, with the long fuse burning ominously. Figuratively speaking, we all understand the predicament. But here's where Paul leaves many of us behind, and makes that turn from despair to joy. Paul's prison experience, even with the deprivation and pain involved, does not create in him self-pity or complaint. Instead, with Christ's help, Paul makes of his situation a positive metaphor. He is an "ambassador [for the gospel] in chains" (Eph. 6:20). He stresses that, as he is bound in prison, so should his congregation be "bound in peace" (compare Eph. 4:3; 6:15, 23) by its faith in Christ, who has freed us from the captivity of sin and death to be "joined" as a common body.

Paul's is a remarkable vision. When Christians are joined together, they find strength rather than distress. They will be stronger together because they are together in Christ. It's when they split up that they get into trouble.

Verse 4:12, "to equip the saints for the work of ministry, for building up the body of Christ," is well known in contemporary studies of parish ministry. A bewildering number of texts and "paradigms" have appeared over the years on the interrelated topics of parish leadership, church volunteerism, and the "equipping" and "liberation" of the laity. Laity should be given permission to lead and minister; they shouldn't have to butt against parish bureaucracy and entrenched, change-resistant thinking. In the spirit of Ephesians 4:12, parish ministers are to equip the laity rather than performing and controlling ministry themselves. They are to help the laity become empowered by the Spirit.

Parish leadership texts vary widely, from the technical to the readable. My favorite is *The Equipping Pastor: A Systems Approach to Congregational Leadership* by R. Paul Stevens and Phil Collins (Alban Institute), because it clearly recognizes the complexity and uniqueness of individual parishes. Other books take God's own work for granted and consider primarily our human efforts. I once browsed through a church growth text and noticed that the author didn't get around to discussing prayer as a factor in congregational ministry until chapter nine. "Should have recognized it at the start!" someone had written in the margin.

Our lesson from Ephesians corrects that unintentional Pelagianism. In the context of the church, what are leadership abilities other than gifts of the Spirit? To treat them as anything else is to miss the whole point. Furthermore, a congregation and its leaders cannot "equip the saints" without also (as Paul puts it) "building up the body of Christ" and encouraging "the unity of faith," "maturity," and "the measure of the full stature of Christ" (v. 13).

Paul's words are good to remember in serving congregations. What is the point of all our committees? Does "ministry of the laity" mean getting a bunch of jobs done (because someone has said they need doing) or, as Paul puts it, does lay ministry mean to "knit together" Christ's body "by every ligament" (v. 16)? How well do the various aspects of the congregation contribute not only to ministry but also (and perhaps especially) to unity, faith, and Christian maturity?

As Christians, we are joined together, responsible for one another's Christian walk and well-being. Paul talks about "one body and one Spirit,...one hope of your calling, one Lord, one faith, one baptism, one God and Father of all" (vv. 4—6a). So when someone we know is in trouble—some metaphorical fuse is burning in his or her life—we're there for that person, praying, talking, listening, and helping. We "bear with one another in love," with "humility, gentleness, and patience" (4:2, cf. Col. 3:12). Of course, it's easier to describe that kind of fellowship with good religious words than actually to pull it off. In a *New Yorker* cartoon fifteen or twenty years ago, the Three Musketeers were crossing their swords together. But instead of saying, "All for one and one for all," they declared, "Every man for himself!" Too often we say "one body" and don't mean it at all. What makes Paul's prison reflections so remarkable is that he isn't thinking primarily of his own drastic situation, or of how he's going to get himself out of his tight spot. Instead, he is thinking of invisible bonds of peace, bonds that are far stronger than any of his chains.

The Jesus Diet

PAUL STROBLE

John 6:35, 41–51; Ephesians 4:25—5:2

Jesus said to them, "I am the bread of life. Whoever comes to me will never be hungry, and whoever believes in me will never be thirsty." (John 6:35)

My father was a cook in the army. Years later, he still cooked as if he were preparing a meal for a division about to take a hill. He believed that food shouldn't be wasted, yet he cooked potfuls of it for a family of three. "Why didn't you like it?" or "What was wrong with it?" he'd say when I could eat only one very large plateful. And when I really did justice to his cooking, he'd brag, "Paul ate six biscuits!" with the same pride as he'd say, "Paul has a master's degree from Yale!"

Then one year my metabolism changed. I was afraid of getting fat, so I started to watch what I ate. I felt as if I were letting Dad down by not eating enough to please him, but I was not so starved for his approval (pun intended) that I would risk becoming overweight.

Family meals at my Grandma Crawford's farm were plenteous, too. A pump at her kitchen sink drew water from a cistern.

An early model refrigerator held bottles of orange soda pop stocked just for me. When our extended family converged, we were joined by cousins, aunts, uncles, and many more. And did we eat! At the kids' table, I made mashed potato and gravy lakes on my plate, then gleefully smashed them with my spoon. After dessert, some of the relatives lingered in the kitchen and cleaned up while others stepped outside to smoke and talk about Vietnam. A few collapsed in front of the black and white television set.

Today that family has dwindled until only my mother, several cousins, and I remain. However well those wonderful meals nourished body and soul, they didn't guarantee immortality.

In John 6:1–15 we read John's version of another great feeding: the "feeding of the five thousand." From that account, we learn that Jesus "cooked up" an enormous meal for an enormous crowd. There was no fried chicken or pies, but apparently there was plenty of fish and bread. Twelve baskets of bread were left over, although apparently everyone gobbled up the fish. (I imagine a hillside covered with fish bones.) Perhaps some paused afterward to discuss the Roman occupation. And surely there was at least one father who announced proudly, "Zedekiah ate six loaves!"

Word got around that Jesus had put little expense and preparation, humanly speaking, into this meal; in fact, the whole feast had appeared from a boy's portion. Naturally the crowd followed him when Jesus headed across the Sea of Galilee to Capernaum. But this time Jesus offered a different type of nourishment. He offered them the bread of life—in other words, himself. In Jesus we have everything we need for life—if we define "life" more broadly than just by our physical needs. Jesus provides God's grace, help, guidance, and assistance. He provides access to God for our prayers. He helps resolve some of our problems and adverse situations. Other situations he does not resolve for us, but even then he remains present for us as we bring our needs to God. He provides us life forever with God.

What do our lives look like when they're sustained by the bread of life? Many times in our churches, we aren't so much nourished by Christ as wearied by preparations. I'm talking not just about potlucks but about all the tasks of ministry. "Sometimes church seems too much like work," sighed a friend one Sunday morning, as she hurried to locate people for committee business. Pastors and lay leaders know that feeling. We become satiated by work and not quite filled by the bread and drink that satisfies us spiritually. We remain as needy as ever, and wearied by our efforts.

But when our lives are fed by Jesus' living bread, they begin to look like those Paul described in Ephesians. Then we attend to our words. We manage our anger. We work not only for our own needs but are mindful of others' needs and generous in responding to them. We encourage and forgive one another. We put away those things like "bitterness and wrath and anger and wrangling and slander…and malice" (Eph. 4:31), and pattern our lives on God's attitude toward us. Add other "fruits of the Spirit" to the mix, and we have a good picture of a person nourished by Christ and prepared by the Holy Spirit.

As we read in Ephesians 5:1–2, "Be imitators of God, as beloved children, and live in love, as Christ loved us and gave himself up for us, a fragrant offering and sacrifice to God." This was not enough for the crowds that followed Jesus, of course. Like the Israelites who complained of hunger to Moses, Jesus' opponents complained about him. One can't help but sympathize with them a little. He was speaking eucharistically before there was a eucharist, and his intimacy with God seemed blasphemous.

Yet even these first hearers, though disgusted by his talk of eating flesh, could understand other parts of his message. God has become clear in the person of Jesus. God approves us, gently draws us to Christ, and teaches us. God has taken full initiative to provide sustenance sufficient for this life and the next. God does not even fret about how much we eat; God simply invites us to his well-stocked table of abundant blessing. As it was for those early listeners, so it is for us.

Don't Be Ridiculous

JOHN ORTBERG

John 6:51–58; Ephesians 5:15–20

So do not be foolish, but understand what the will of the Lord is. (Ephesians 5:17)

In Garrison Keillor's mythical Lake Wobegon, Pastor Ingqvist is alarmed when he glances at Dear Abby columns and notices how often she refers her readers to ministers. Talk to your minister, Abby counsels a fourteen–year-old deeply in love with a fifty–something married man serving serious time in a federal penitentiary.

> [A]s she pours out her love for Vince, her belief in his innocence, the fact that his wife never loved him…not like she, Trish, can love him, and the fact that despite his age and their never having met except in letters, there is something indescribably sacred and precious between them; all the pastor can think is: "You're crazy. Don't be ridiculous."

Thou shalt not be ridiculous. Paul says, "See then that ye walk circumspectly, not as fools but as wise, redeeming the time, because the days are evil" (Eph. 5:15–16, KJV). When Paul wrote that wonderful sentence he probably was sitting in an upper room in Athens. It was late at night, quiet, and all the fools were asleep. He could write the simple truth, and no fool was around to say, "Huh? What do you mean? Are you saying I shouldn't go for the world long-distance walking-backward record? But I can do it! I can walk backward for miles."

One of the marks of the human condition is that it is not simply depraved or lost; it is also ridiculous. Paul says that as we relate to each other we are to sing psalms and hymns and spiritual songs, making melody to the Lord in our hearts and giving thanks to God at all times. But even in the church we end up spending more time fighting about the kind of melodies we should sing, and whether the Lord God prefers organ or guitar. People split churches over how loudly the songs should be amplified. We are ridiculous.

Things are no better outside. Imagine what the world might be like if CEOs of large corporations would go into Watts or Cabrini Green and sing and make melody in their hearts. Or if Israelis and Palestinians spent a day singing psalms and hymns to one another. When we are alone at night and all the fools are asleep, it is not hard to imagine such a world. But why does it remain so ridiculously remote?

Of course, folly in the tradition of ancient wisdom literature involves something more tragic than wasting energy trying to get into the *Guinness Book of World Records*. Foolishness, in this way of thinking, is not so much a disease of the intellect as of the will. The fool says in her heart that there is no God; or that she will live as god, which is perhaps the same thing. The fool thinks he needs bigger barns for the riches that he in his cleverness has accumulated, and forgets that the night when his construction project is finished is the night he has scheduled a massive coronary. You can be a fool and still find good work in Cambridge, Massachusetts, or on Madison Avenue. Sometimes it helps.

Paul said of fools: "Their god is their stomach" (Phil. 3:19, NIV). They have a philosophy of life that was perhaps best articulated by *Sesame Street*'s Cookie Monster: "See cookie. Want cookie. Absorb cookie. Seek ye first the cookie." Some of the highest-IQ people in our world stay up late at night trying to find new ways to convince us that we are nothing more than a collection of appetites. See. Want. Absorb. What would Paul say to a society whose magazine covers feature well-coiffed, aerobicized versions of the Cookie Monster? "Thou shalt not be ridiculous."

Scholars tell us that the ancient Hebrews had a fierce appetite for wisdom. They loved wisdom so much that they spoke of her as a person: "Does not wisdom call out? Does not understanding raise her voice?…Listen to me: happy are those who keep my ways…For whoever finds me finds life" (Prov. 8). They hoped for the coming of wisdom as we hope for the resurrection of the NASDAQ.

Then wisdom became a person. He came so that hungry people and thirsty people could finally be filled. (To be hungry and thirsty, Dallas Willard writes, is to be driven by unsatisfied desires. We live in a hungry world.) Wisdom was born in a manger and died on a cross, and in between said that our only shot at ever being filled up is if we follow him in the life of self-emptying love. He said that our only hope for being filled is to be filled with him, to absorb him, to follow in the way of the one who emptied himself and thus became the fullness of all things. See Jesus. Want Jesus. Absorb Jesus.

Paul said for such people a new kind of fullness is possible. "Do not get drunk with wine [that is, don't consider yourself a giant appetite to be gratified]…but be filled with the Spirit" (Eph. 5:18). I grew up in circles in which we stayed far away from wine, and were not all that sure about the Spirit. But it is in the Spirit where true fullness lies, in "the shy member of the Trinity," as Dale Bruner says, the member who is always pointing beyond himself. The fullness of the Spirit comes only when we are emptied of all the ego and self-preoccupation that promises so much and delivers so little; emptied of all that is foolish and dying and ridiculous. It is the Spirit that Jesus was so full of that the life came spilling out of him as well.

Be careful how you live…

Roll Call

JOHN ORTBERG

John 6:56–69; Ephesians 6:10–20

> *Because of this many of his disciples turned back and no
> longer went about with him. So Jesus asked the twelve, "Do
> you also wish to go away?" (John 6:66–67)*

Of all the questions in Scripture, the single most poignant one
may be recorded in the sixth chapter of the gospel of John. Jesus
has just finished giving what is regarded as one of his difficult
sayings (though a friend once asked which of Jesus' sayings is
not difficult). This one spoke of the need for people to eat his flesh
and drink his blood and pointed to the difficulty involved for
anyone who wanted to follow him.

Because of this, the writer says, "many of his disciples turned
back and no longer went about with him." It is striking that John
uses the word *disciples* for those who turn back; these are apparently not just casual listeners, not the folks who show up only at
Christmas and Easter. These people have been teaching Sunday
school and working in the nursery. When longtime pillars start
leaving the church, we get a little restless; people want to bring in
consultants and do focus groups to diagnose the problem.

So Jesus called the Twelve together and put the question to them with unsettling directness: "Do you also wish to go away?"

I wonder how Jesus asked the question. I wonder if there was an edge to it—was he issuing a challenge? I sometimes imagine that he asked it sadly. Maybe he asked it with a sigh, his shoulders sagging a little. Maybe it was hard to see people who had been counted on as followers leave—to see many followers leave. There is something humbling about having to ask such a question.

"Do you also wish to go away?" I wonder sometimes how I would have responded to the question. Because at times the truth is I do wish to go away. I don't like thinking this about myself. But in times of temptation, in times when I deceive other people to avoid trouble or get what I want, in times when I deliberately close my eyes to the sight of those who are poor or marginalized because I don't want to feel guilty or bother to help, I too am one of the ones who wish to go away.

Do you also wish to go away? Peter's response is striking. He doesn't say "yes," of course, but he doesn't quite say "no" either. Instead, in good Jesus-style, he answers back with another question: "To whom [else] can we go?" (6:68). It is not, perhaps, the most flattering answer in the world, but it is honest. It's a little reminiscent of Winston Churchill's famous description of democracy as the worst form of government except for every other form that has ever been tried. Following Jesus may not always be easy, or pleasant, or even totally comprehensible; but when it comes to the eternal-life business, to tell the truth there's not much out there in the way of alternatives.

As ethicist Lewis Smedes said, "This is where the trolley stops…Without Jesus we are stuck with two options: utopian illusion or deadly despair. I scorn illusion. I dread despair. So I put all my money on Jesus."

"Do you also wish to go away?" The young church at Ephesus is struggling to maintain its existence when the worship of Artemis or Caesar or Mammon is a much more attractive alternative. Paul ends a letter to the Ephesians with an extended metaphor that sounds violently unattractive in our day: "Put on the whole armor of God, so that you may be able to stand against the wiles of the devil" (Eph. 6:11).

Apparently Paul did not expect following Jesus to be easy. He talks about the life of those in the church as if it's going to be a kind of war. Ben Patterson writes that no soldier ever exclaimed in hurt tones during a battle: "Hey—they're shooting at me." Getting shot at is more or less what you expect when you sign up.

Paul, however, knew that the citizens of Ephesus saw helmets and breastplates, shields and swords, every day. Rome did not always speak softly, but it carried a big stick. Paul tells everyone to gear up for battle, but it is a different kind of battle. It is marked by truth—which is the first casualty of war. Its advance is marked by salvation—healing and wholeness, rather than body bags. Its gospel—its good news, the headlines of the PR department—is peace. Walter Brueggemann has written that the ancient texts of scripture can be read as subversive material, as a way for those without power to undermine and conspire against the damage being done by the "rulers and authorities." Few texts are more subversive than Paul's words at the end of this letter.

"Do you also wish to go away?" Jim Wallis writes that when the South African government canceled a political rally against apartheid, Desmond Tutu led a worship service in St. George's Cathedral. The walls were lined with soldiers and riot police carrying guns and bayonets, ready to close it down. Bishop Tutu began to speak of the evils of the apartheid system—how the rulers and authorities that propped it up were doomed to fail. He pointed a finger at the police who were there to record his words: "You may be powerful—very powerful—but you are not God. God cannot be mocked. You have already lost."

Then, in a moment of unbearable tension, the bishop seemed to soften. Coming out from behind the pulpit, he flashed that radiant Tutu smile and began to bounce up and down with glee. "Therefore, since you have already lost, we are inviting you to join the winning side."

The crowd roared, the police melted away, and the people began to dance. Don't go away, Paul says. Put on your armor and dance. I am inviting you to join the winning side.

Pharisees Are Us

JOHN ORTBERG

Mark 7:1–8, 21–23

*"You abandon the commandment of God and hold to human
tradition." (Mark 7:8)*

I grew up in an era before video, *Veggie Tales,* or Bible-based com-
puter games. I was raised, at least in terms of religious education,
on the flannel graph. To this day, although I know that the
scriptures are peopled with characters of texture and nuance, I
think Bible people and see pastel paper figures pressed on a felt
board.

Perhaps the most flattened characters were the Pharisees. They
were presented as foils against which the virtue of New Testament
heroes stood out in sharp relief. When the Pharisees got into a
fight with Jesus over hand-washing, the flannel graph reduced
the story to a simple battle of bizarre legalism and a Lady Macbeth–
like obsession with purity versus simple, sanctified common sense.
We all knew whose side we would have been on.

But over the past few decades, we've learned that things were
not quite that simple. Gregory Peck, not long before he died, said
that if you're going to play the part of the devil you have to look

for the angel in him, and if you're going to play an angel you have to look for the devil in him—a kind of actor's "hermeneutic of charity." We may need to do this with flannel graph characters. What else might have been going on in Mark's chapter 7 besides a simple contest between legalism and common sense?

James Dunn notes that in the first century a disproportionate amount of rabbinic attention was devoted to three areas of the law: dietary rules, Sabbath-keeping, and circumcision. This was in spite of the fact that rabbis would not have claimed these as the central aspects of God's will for humanity. They knew that the essence of the law was the *shema*—the loving of God with heart and soul and strength. So why the relentless focus on dietary laws, circumcision, and Sabbath-keeping?

The answer, Dunn says, involves "identity markers," or boundaries. All groups of human beings have a tendency to be exclusive; they want to know who is inside and who is out. So they adopt identity markers—visible practices of dress or vocabulary or behavior that serve to distinguish who is inside the group from who is outside.

For instance, if you were driving along in the '60s and saw a Volkswagen van plastered with "Make Love Not War" bumper stickers, with a long-haired, tie-dyed, granny-glasses-wearing driver, you'd know you were observing a hippie. If it was the '80s and you saw a BMW driver wearing Gucci shoes and a Rolex watch, you'd know you were observing a yuppie. Every fraternity or sorority has its own uniform.

With this in mind, the attention given to the purity codes in the first century becomes clearer. As Tom Wright says: "The Temple cult, and the observance of Sabbaths, of food taboos, and of circumcision were the key things which marked out Jew from gentile, which maintained and reinforced exactly the agenda, both political and religious, of the hard-line Pharisees."

Jesus is not accusing the Pharisees of an early form of Pelagianism, of trying to earn their justification by strenuous moral effort. He does not regard these laws as bizarre or outlandish. Perhaps most important, he does not reject his own religious culture. He agrees with the Pharisees that God's work in human history is happening precisely through the life and destiny of this people of Israel.

But now, he says, the kingdom is breaking into human history in a new and unexpected way. It means the end for the "kingdom of the gentiles," although the kingdom of God will triumph not by "paying back the gentiles in their own coin," as Wright says, but by turning the other cheek and walking the second mile. The identity markers that will proclaim the authenticity of the people of God will be a circumcised heart and a diet of justice and love. Then people will not simply try to do right things; they will be the kind of persons who want to do right things; they will be clean "inside." Jesus saw this not as the repudiation of Israel's ancient dream, but as its ultimate fulfillment.

Here is where Jesus' words become as convicting in our day as they were to the Pharisees, for the struggle of Mark 7 is a struggle inside every human being who seeks to take faith seriously. There is a self-righteousness in me that does not want to die. There is something inside me that is not bothered when others are excluded, that wants others to be excluded, that feels more special when I'm on the inside and somebody else is not. There was something in me—even when I was young—that enjoyed looking at the flannel graph and thinking about how much wiser and more loved by God I was than those foolish, exclusive Pharisees.

Henri Nouwen wrote that it is very hard to stop being the prodigal son without turning into the elder brother. Any time people are not experiencing authentic transformation—as in Mark 7:21–23—they will inevitably be drawn toward some kind of faith characterized by boundary markers. We will look for substitute ways of distinguishing ourselves from those on the outside. The boundary markers change from century to century, but they all reinforce a false sense of superiority, fed by the intent to exclude others.

Ironically, the one human being who was perfectly free from self-righteousness is the only one who was completely righteous. The least exclusive member of the human race is also its most exalted. The only person who has ever been truly free of a messiah complex was the Messiah.

True Grit

JOHN ORTBERG

(Matthew 15:21–28); Mark 7:24–37; James 2:1–10

But she answered him, "Sir, even the dogs under the table eat the children's crumbs." (Mark 7:28)

When I was in first grade, teachers assigned students to reading groups based on how well they could read. They would name all the groups after birds so that everyone would feel equal, but you could always tell how well you were doing by what bird your group was named after. There were the Eagles, the Robins, and the Pigeons. The Pigeons were not reading *War and Peace*.

Ken Bailey gives a wonderful treatment of Mark's story about Jesus' encounter with the Syro-Phoenician woman in his comment on the parallel passage in Matthew. To grasp the point, Bailey says, it is helpful to think of it as a kind of test given simultaneously to two sets of people, the woman and the disciples. Watch who ends up in the Pigeons group.

Matthew tells us that the woman approaches Jesus with the traditional cry of a beggar: "Have mercy on me" (Mt. 15:22). She humbles herself and adds the title "Lord"—a term she will repeat twice more. She calls him "Son of David"—she knows something of Judaism and is deeply respectful.

Jesus does not say a word. Matthew deliberately draws our attention to this point. This woman's daughter is suffering terribly, but when the woman appeals to Jesus with humility and reverence, he acts as if he doesn't hear.

She must decide if she's willing to persevere.

Meanwhile, Bailey says, Jesus is testing the disciples. He ignores the woman to see what they will do. "Send her away," they say, "She keeps shouting after us" (v. 23b). They are exaggerating a little—there's no indication the woman approached them. But they're confident Jesus will do what they say.

"I was sent only to the lost sheep of...Israel" (v. 24), Jesus responds, apparently agreeing with them. "I was sent to Israel, God's favorites." Good call. Let's send her away.

Only he doesn't send her away, but watches the disciples to see how they will respond. Will any of his students understand that many are coming "from the east and the west"? Will anyone say a word on behalf of the woman?

No. They all nod their heads.

The woman will not go away. In her mind she can hear her daughter's screams. Maybe it is desperation. Maybe it is trust. She kneels on the ground and utters a single phrase: "Lord, help me" (v. 25c).

Now the tension in the disciples starts to build. Their theology tells them this woman is to be shunned, rejected. They would say just the same thing Jesus did.

And yet...they listen to the anguished plea of a heartsick mother for a suffering child. Something in them is moved—something must have been moved. This is striking at deep assumptions about whom God loves. Could it be that God is better than their theology?

Jesus speaks again—it may be that he is still facing the disciples. "It is not fair to take the children's food and throw it to the dogs" (v. 26). Dogs were regarded as unclean scavengers, little better than pigs. The meaning is clear. Jesus is giving voice to their theology. It is one thing to have contempt for someone behind his or her back. It is another thing to hear the ugliness of our thoughts and feelings expressed out loud to a real human being.

Will any of them speak up for her? Will one of them love her? No. Not today. There will be other tests in days to come, and they will do better. But not today.

Jesus turns to the woman. Bailey notes that of the two primary words available for dog, Matthew selects *kunariois*—a little dog, a "doggette"—to soften what he says to the woman.

Still, her response is unbelievable. "Yes, Lord," she says, calling him Lord for the third time. "Yet even the dogs eat the crumbs that fall from their masters' table." She picks up on the diminutive form of the word *dogs* and uses the same form for the word *crumbs*: "even the little doggettes get the little crumbettes from their master's table." Here is a woman who comes back at Jesus with grit, grace, even wit. She has an attitude. "You are still my Lord and master. Go ahead and make it look like you're pushing me away. I'm not going anywhere. By all means, feed the kids. But I bet you have a crumb even for me. I bet you do."

She just won't give up.

Finally Jesus turns to face the woman. Finally the mask is off. For a moment Jesus conceals the great goodness of his heart, but that moment is quickly past. The test is over. She's aced the final.

"Woman," he says, "Great is your faith" (v. 28).

The disciples look on in astonishment. This woman—their enemy, their inferior—has been given one of the greatest commendations ever bestowed by the one whom they follow so closely. It turns out that they—who thought they basked in the exclusivity of what C. S. Lewis called the "Inner Ring"—belong in the Pigeon reading group. And this pagan Gentile woman is one of the Eagles.

"My brothers [and sisters], as believers in our glorious Lord Jesus Christ, don't show favoritism" (Jas. 2:1, NIV), writes James. Jesus' followers are still tested in offices and cubicles, at school desks and cafeterias, at the boundary lines between nations, races, and cultures, around breakfast tables and family rooms.

The story of this woman shows what we are all so slow to grasp: that the most desirable society in the cosmos turns out to be the humblest. Father, Son, and Spirit are determined that the circle of love they share from all eternity should be ceaselessly, shamelessly inclusive. None are left out except those who refuse to enter.

Lesson Plans

MARY E. HINKLE

Mark 8:27–38; James 3:1–12

*Not many of you should become teachers, my brothers and
sisters, for you know that we who teach will be judged with
greater strictness. (James 3:1)*

With fall education programs getting under way and Sunday
school teachers beginning another year of teaching, it may be
disconcerting to hear this reading from James: "Not many of you
should become teachers, my brothers and sisters, for you know
that we who teach will be judged with greater strictness."

In this chapter James is warning his listeners that it is difficult
to guard the tongue. But the link between the first verse and the
rest of the chapter is not self-evident. Why begin this section by
addressing teachers? Is self-control with respect to words harder
for teachers than others? (No fair answering if you are in academic
administration.) Or is it just that teachers, like preachers, make
their living with words, and so the likelihood of error is greater
for them? With access to so much rope, it is only a matter of time
before we professional speakers hang ourselves.

Yet I wonder if both of these answers aren't beside the point that James is making. In the first two chapters of the letter, James points out instances of hypocrisy. When we say we have faith but do not care for the widow and orphan, what kind of faith are we confessing? Who exactly are we saying we believe in? Surely not the God of Abraham, Rahab, and Jesus (Jas. 2:23–26). It is hypocrisy when our speech and actions are not in sync. When we show favoritism to the rich and send the poor away empty, we are falsifying any statement of faith we make in the God of our Lord Jesus.

It is also hypocrisy when speech (in one context) and speech (in another) are not in sync, and this is the problem James addresses. If we bless the Creator God and then curse someone created in the image of God, we not only say something unfavorable about another human being. We also say something untrue about God— namely, that God makes junk. We are professing a theology of creation opposed to the testimony that "God saw everything that he had made, and indeed, it was very good" (Gen. 1:31). One element of our speech gives the lie to the other, and in the end we are not just lying; we are lying about God. Hence the strict judgment. The warning James gives is especially for those who— by virtue of praying, praising, preaching, or just talking about God—are teachers of divine things.

Maybe this is why Jesus becomes so angry with Peter. When Peter rejects Jesus' teaching that the Messiah must be crucified, Peter is beginning to fashion a lie about God. Surely, Peter is suggesting, there must be an easier way.

I would very much like for Peter to be right, for I have never understood why God needed the bloody sacrifice of an innocent victim to forgive sin. Why couldn't Jesus have just kept on healing people and telling parables and blessing children until, at an advanced age, he died in his sleep? Or aged gracefully as a teacher, spending summers at the lake, sporting a neatly trimmed salt-and-pepper beard, and greeting class after class of ever younger, fresh-faced disciples every fall? "Consider the lilies of the field...," he would say, and pens would start scribbling across the pages of notebooks.

"Then he began to teach them that the Son of Man must undergo great suffering, and be rejected by the elders, the chief priests, and the scribes, and be killed, and after three days rise again" (Mk. 8:31). Peter doesn't agree. Surely there is an easier way!

But although Peter's teaching career starts out innocently enough (according to Matthew, Peter says, "This must never happen to you" [Mt. 16:22c]), look where it leads. Before long, Peter is face to face with the prospect of his own great suffering, which he averts only by his passionate testimony, "I do not know the man!" (Mt. 26:72, 74). There is an easier way, and Peter finds it, but only by lying about his association with the one he has known and confessed to be God's anointed.

Perhaps, then, Jesus "must suffer" because he will not lie about whether and how he knows God. The Son of Man must suffer because he will reject every compromise with the authorities, the crowds, the Romans, and even with his own beloved Peter. Although it is true that "for God all things are possible" (Mt. 19:26; Mk. 10:27; 14:36), it is hard to speak truth to power and then spend summers at the lake. Jesus will speak truth to power, and power will squash him like a gnat.

I was recently part of a small focus group that offered feedback on a newly designed Web site for the seminary where I teach. We talked for a while about the colors, the graphics, the menus and submenus, and then one of the group members said, "Nowhere on these pages is there a cross." She was right. I was surprised, but even more stunned and chastened by the realization that I had not even noticed its absence. I wondered where else we were not clearly saying, "Look, you need to know this man died. He was tortured and executed. It was awful."

Where else—as congregations, as schools, as teachers—are we not saying this? As we manage to tell the story of Jesus without the cross, we have learned what Peter was teaching as he took Jesus aside and began to rebuke him. As we follow Peter's teaching and repeat it, Jesus may find a way to say to us, as he said to Peter, "Get behind me, Satan! For you are setting your mind not on divine things but on human things" (Mk. 8:33b). This is the strictness with which teachers will be judged.

Seeing Things

MARY E. HINKLE

Mark 9:30–37

> *"Whoever welcomes one such child in my name welcomes me,*
> *and whoever welcomes me welcomes not me but the one who*
> *sent me." (Mark 9:37)*

"Start seeing motorcycles," said the bumper sticker. I didn't know I wasn't seeing motorcycles, I thought, then realized that that was the point. How do you begin to see something you didn't know you were missing?

"Start seeing the resurrection," says Jesus, as he walks with the disciples to Jerusalem. He is teaching them about his death and resurrection, but they don't understand. They are confused and reluctant to ask for clarification. Perhaps they're afraid of looking stupid again. After all, the last time they thought they understood what Jesus was talking about, he was warning them about the Pharisees and Herod, and they were thinking about bread (Mk. 8:14–21). *Oops.* Or maybe they are frightened into silence by the words "betrayed" and "killed." Whatever the cause of their fear, they do not respond to Jesus when he describes the end of their journey.

Instead, as the walk progresses, the disciples find their way into a discussion about which of them is the greatest. They are graduate students comparing GRE scores. They are ministers discussing how many they worship each week, as in, "We worship about 450 at both services." They are anyone who has ever written a memo containing the words "measurable outcomes." Which of the disciples is the star pupil? Who is the greatest?

It is easy to portray the disciples as self-involved here, but maybe that is unfair. What if the outcome they were trying to measure was faithfulness to their teacher? What if they were arguing about who really understood Jesus, including what Jesus was saying about his death? We know they were confused by his passion predictions. We know, too, that they are not the only followers to wonder what exactly is required of one who seeks to remain faithful to Jesus. Maybe the conversation about greatness grew out of a conversation about what it really meant for them to stay beside Jesus all the way to Jerusalem.

The way of the cross is no less confounding or frightening today. Because of this, it is fashionable in some circles to speak of Christianity as a set of skills that one learns to practice, the way one learns the skills necessary to be a woodworker or a research chemist. New pastors are advised to find the masters of Christianity in their parish and apprentice themselves to these giants of Christian practice. And if we are going to apprentice ourselves to a master, we must learn who is the greatest.

Which brings us back to the disciples on the road. Unfortunately, inside the house in Capernaum, Jesus is unimpressed by the disciples' tidy argument about their need to know who is the greatest. He looks around for help to make his point. He sits down, calls his pupils to sit around him and begins to teach by bringing a child into the group. We don't know if the child was a girl or a boy. (The Greek word for child is gender neutral.) The vocabulary echoes the culture's view of children. To almost all adults, and certainly to adult male disciples focused on their alpha male teacher and their measurable likeness to him, children were of no consequence. Children were invisible.

In Luke 7, a Pharisee is scandalized when Jesus allows a woman, a known sinner, to wash his feet and anoint them with ointment. Jesus asks him, "Do you see this woman?" (Lk. 7:44). Something similar is happening when Jesus stands a child up in the midst of his disciples, then takes the child in his arms the way Simeon had once embraced baby Jesus and says, "Whoever welcomes one such child in my name welcomes me, and whoever welcomes me welcomes not me but the one who sent me" (Mk. 9:37). The disciples want to know who is the best at following Jesus, and Jesus says, "Do you see this child?" As Pheme Perkins observes, "This example treats the child, who was socially invisible, as the stand-in for Jesus."

In one of Sue Grafton's mysteries, the murderer turns out to be a sixty–year-old woman who is thirty pounds overweight. After the mystery is solved, the detective reflects that the woman nearly got away with murder simply because no one would remember seeing someone like her. Nothing about her made her noticeable. She was, for all practical purposes, invisible.

So it was with a child in antiquity. Jesus sees something the disciples do not even know they are missing.

This gospel text's bumper sticker might be, "Start seeing the invisible." Start seeing the invisible, not because it is virtuous to do so, not so that we can congratulate ourselves on being the greatest at seeing. Start seeing the invisible because to receive the invisible one is to receive Jesus, and to receive Jesus is to receive the one who sent him.

Where is the invisible Jesus who will teach you the way of the cross? Will you learn to pray from the "masters," the saints in your community, the old faithful ones? Probably you will. But there is also that panicked woman in the ICU waiting room who has never prayed, and who teaches you to pray when she clenches her hands to her forehead and says, "God, please!" Do you see her?

You may learn to preach from the tapes of great preachers, and refine your theology by reading the writings of seminary professors. But a teenager near you could be a preacher too, one with a talent for testimony that you've never seen. The most solid sacramental theology you hear this week may come from the five-year-old who tells you she thinks she is ready to receive communion because, simply, "I can eat." If you see them, you see Jesus.

At Ground Zero

STEPHEN PAUL BOUMAN

James 5:13–20

> *Are any among you suffering? They should pray. Are*
> *any cheerful? They should sing songs of praise. Are*
> *any among you sick? They should call for the elders*
> *of the church and have them pray over them, anointing*
> *them with oil in the name of the Lord.*
> *(James 5:13–14)*

I looked down at the familiar face of a young woman dying of
AIDS. Her breathing was ragged, her eyes closed. Ramona was a
leader of her struggling inner-city church, with an infectious and
earthy love of her Lord. She had become a friend in the Diakonia
lay training program, and at some point we had switched roles:
she became the teacher and I the student.

Her struggle with her illness was also a struggle of faith. She
had shared much of it with me: her anger and struggle to forgive
her husband, whose intravenous drug use had visited this disease
on her; her worry about her children and her parents; her elation
and depression as she rode the rhythms of AIDS; her determination

to maintain a strong interior landscape as her body deteriorated; her daily search for Jesus in all of it; her anguish at the swath this disease was cutting through the black community.

Now she was too weak to speak, but nodded her head toward my communion set. The faith is never more carnal and touching than when we are in the presence of suffering or illness. We proceeded with what Father Divine called the "tangibillification" of God. I communed her with the tiniest bit of wafer, anointed her head with oil, and prayed for God's healing presence. We shared a blessing. I sat down and held her hand.

"I would like to give you a gift," her father said to me from his chair in the corner. He rose and in a deep voice recited a poem titled "Heaven's Grocery Store." He gestured, his voice rising and falling dramatically as he became consumed by his poem, oblivious to those who stopped by the door to listen. His gift to me for caring about his daughter was also his way of telling her that heaven awaited her.

With a nod of her head, Ramona had confessed her faith. With a poem from his oral tradition, her father confessed his. In a hospital room in Bayonne, New Jersey, two children of God made the church's ancient confession their present quiet joy. "Are any cheerful? They should sing songs of praise." The pastor lay in bed in a Brooklyn hospital, fighting the last stages of brain cancer. We spoke of many things, but the conversation repeatedly returned to the people and ministry of the Bronx congregation where he had served as interim pastor. His gently loving and patient pastoral ministry had helped the parish grasp a hopeful vision of the future. Their history of conflict and heartbreaking decline had many wondering if there was any future for this parish. His ministry provided space for healing and reconciliation. He loved the people of the parish back into confidence in their giftedness and potential. In the hospital bed this pastor spoke of his love for Fordham Lutheran Church in the Bronx.

Again the carnal "tangibillification" of the church. Bread and wine. "The Lord be with you...lift up your heart" echoing the prayers and songs of generations of faith. Oil traced on a sweaty, fevered forehead, reminding us of baptism and healing presence. It was like a revelation to this pastor. He ate and drank and was touched by oil, and he gave me a knowing smile. "So," he said, "This is what I have been doing."

"Are any among you sick? They should call for the elders of the church and have them pray over them, anointing them with oil in the name of the Lord."

Members of his congregation gathered frequently at his bedside. They sang his favorite hymns, prayed, shared favorite passages from scripture. By their faith and presence, they reminded him of resurrection hope. The pastor whom God had sent to heal the heartbreak in the life of this parish was now visited in his own vulnerability at the gate of death. "Are any among you suffering? They should pray." We watched in horror from our sixteenth-floor office window on that day in 2001, as both towers of the World Trade Center lit up, then fell into a cloud of smoke and ash. Then we gathered in the chapel of the Interchurch Center with hundreds who came to pray, not knowing the fate of loved ones. I asked the people to name the folks in their hearts and their concern as our prayer before God. The chapel rang out with the precious names of loved ones, spoken through clenched teeth, strained and breaking voices.

Sitting next to a soot-covered survivor on a bench who was screaming hysterically as bodies rained from the sky, a pastor's wife (who had just escaped from Tower One) takes her hand and quotes Romans 8:39b—"[Nothing can] separate us from the love of God in Christ Jesus our Lord."

A chaplain anointed the foreheads of firefighters with oil. Later survivors remembered seeing glistening foreheads rushing past them toward rescue…and death, living out baptismal vocation.

At Ground Zero, breathing lightly through my mask, I searched for hope. Then this came to me like a gift: we are already buried. "Therefore we have been buried with [Christ Jesus] by baptism into death, so that, just as Christ was raised from the dead by the glory of [God], so we too might walk in newness of life" (Rom. 6:4).

Carnal grace.

Jacob's Ladder

STEPHEN PAUL BOUMAN

Hebrews 1:1–4; 2:5–12

> *"What are human beings that you are mindful of them,*
> *or mortals, that you care for them?*
> *You have made them for a little while lower than the angels;*
> *you have crowned them with glory and honor…"*
> *(Hebrews 2:6–7)*

An incredible respect for life wove together the disparate humanity that worked the edges of the New York abyss following September 11, 2001. Iron workers, emergency and fire department rescue teams, volunteers sharing coffee and backrubs, chaplains bending low to listen, gawking tourists, stricken loved ones hunched over pictures and lit candles—all were woven together in the solidarity of citizenship of those regarded by God as "for a little while lower than the angels."

As I arrived one November day to conduct the memorial service for fireman Vincent, all the streets were blocked by fire engines and police vehicles. Vincent had finished his shift at Ladder 35 on the West Side on the morning of September 11 and was on his way home when the first plane hit. He returned and worked on "Jacob's ladder" in the smoky stairways of the towers, ascending and descending as part of a human chain of rescue, suffering, and death. The pastoral task in these latter days has been to grasp the vision of God at each end of the ladder, bearing with us on earth, bearing home those who ascended.

"But we do see Jesus, who for a little while was made lower than the angels, now crowned with glory and honor because of the suffering of death, so that by the grace of God he might taste death for everyone" (Heb. 2:9).

The writer of Hebrews gives us a glimpse into the pastoral life of the early church, living at the far side of the Ground Zero of the paschal mystery: Christ has died; Christ is risen; Christ will come again. On that November day we plumbed the mystery of death and resurrection. As more than one thousand people arrived, the modest parish in Middle Village, Queens, was suddenly in the public eye, handling press, protocol, and immense crowds of distraught people. And this was only one of thousands of memorials held in that season throughout the metropolis.

Many were not accustomed to being in church. Those of us who could sing sang the liturgy on behalf of those who no longer knew the words or were too numb with grief to sing. But that is our theological task. We have been ordained and baptized for these latter days and for a time such as this. How shall we speak and act "in many and various ways"? Pastor Longan remembered the heroic way in which Vinnie lived and died, then moved from Vinnie to God, whose rescue of the world from sin, death, and the evil one was accomplished by the cross and the laid-down life.

"Long ago God spoke to our ancestors in many and various ways by the prophets, but in these last days he has spoken to us by a Son" (Heb. 1:1–2a).

How do we make the great "hand-me-down" of the tradition of faith relevant? After 9/11 people aren't only asking, "What, really, is a Muslim?" They also want to know what a Christian is, and a Christian community. Who is my neighbor now? What does a life worth living look like? Where is true security? What happens when I die? I sense a true desire to learn how to talk to our Maker.

Paul Tillich reminds us that "theology, as a function of the Christian church, must serve the needs of the church. A theological system is supposed to satisfy two basic needs: the statement of the truth of the Christian message and the interpretation of this truth for every new generation."

Vinnie's father got lost in the eulogy. He was fully engaged as he mentioned one memory after another, but then he could not get out of the cul-de-sac of memory. Every time he began to conclude he was unable to face the terrible truth. Vinnie died. And there was not even a body in the church, only the memories.

"As it is we do not yet see everything in subjection to them, but we do see Jesus…" (Heb. 2:8b–9a).

Like Vinnie's father we cannot see the outcome of all things. But at the eucharist we could see and taste Jesus. At the table the truth is told. Christ has died. Vinnie has died. We say it and face it. Christ has risen. Vinnie has been buried with Christ by baptism unto death, so that as Christ was raised from the dead by the power of the Father, so Vinnie will again walk in newness of life. Christ will come again, and bring us home where Vinnie waits with angels and archangels and all the company of heaven…in every time and every place.

Two months after the memorial service they found Vinnie's remains. Silence washed over Ground Zero. Hats were removed, bodies waited reverently as they lifted him from the wreckage and carried him out. Several days later I attended the liturgy, which centered on Good Friday and a performance of Bach's "St. Matthew's Passion." The church was overflowing, and when the congregation sang, "Lord, let at last thine angels come," we knew that once again in these latter days God had spoken to us.

"It was fitting that God, for whom and through whom all things exist, in bringing many children to glory, should make the pioneer of their salvation perfect through sufferings. For the one who sanctifies and those who are sanctified all have one Father. For this reason Jesus is not ashamed to call them brothers and sisters" (Heb. 2:10–11).

Confirming Erik

STEPHEN PAUL BOUMAN

Hebrews 4:12–16

Since, then, we have a great high priest who has passed through the heavens, Jesus, the Son of God, let us hold fast to our confession. (Hebrews 4:14)

When Erik confessed his faith on the festival of Pentecost, the entire family of believers watched and strained to hear his confession. His chubby fingers were surprisingly dexterous as he signed the words, although he also spoke, as if what he was signing was bursting through the silence of his deafness. This is what he said on the day of his confirmation: "For God so loved the world that he gave his only Son, so that everyone who believes in him may not perish but may have eternal life" (Jn. 3:16).

He paused, fished a card from the pocket beneath his robe, glanced at it, and put it back. Then he continued in his combination of sign language and garbled verbal speech: "What does this mean to me? It means that Jesus died for my sins. It means God loves me. It means when I die I will go to heaven."

He smiled nervously and returned to his place in the line of confirmands. Then he looked at me, passed his hand over his head, and rolled his eyes in a sigh of relief.

The moment bore witness to the grace of a God who brings light from darkness, life from death, speech from silence (compare 1 John 2:7-11; 3:13-22). We call the process of forming Erik's faith catechesis. The partnership between the home and the church, the sheer effort by all involved in Erik's catechesis, is a parable of confessional witness in a culture indifferent or hostile to an active and living Word. The book of Hebrews gives us a glimpse into the pastoral and evangelical life of another confessional witness. What was the organizing principle in the early church? What was expected of converts? What sustained their faith? What was at the center of the early Christian movement?

Several years ago Erik was slipping into a lifetime of silence, becoming progressively more morose and combative as his isolation deepened. His mother began to fight for her son, first against a local public school system that takes a cookie-cutter approach to children, then against the county and state. She won on many fronts through her persistence. Erik entered appropriate programs and began to learn. She learned sign language. He learned to read.

She enrolled him in a Sunday school for the deaf in an Episcopal church and found materials that gave appropriate sign language for religious concepts and vocabulary. How many mothers like Erik's, in the time of the early church, became models of the great high priest, whose solidarity with us in all things human inspired bold witness and teaching of the paschal mystery?

When it was time for Erik's catechesis, his mother and I worked out a home tutoring schedule. Each Wednesday we sat around the dining room table. His mother interpreted. I learned some sign language so that we could communicate the chief parts of Luther's catechism. We had to match theological concepts to Erik's signs, and our catechesis was filled with analogy, story, wild gestures, his mother's manual continuo as she translated our efforts into Erik's language. I tracked the looks of consternation on Erik's face until they reflected the joy of recognition. When he grasped a concept, he would read it back to us in sign and agitated verbalizing. Sin was "bad things" or "bad relationship." I taught the sixth commandment as "Don't have sex unless you are married." The ninth and tenth commandments became "Be happy with what God has given you." You get the idea.

Erik's catechesis was a communal matter of greatest importance. His father would come home from work and join us at the table for a report of his son's progress. Erik's brother would watch the dog and do his homework. On Erik's big day, family, Sunday school teachers, and neighbors joined him at church.

The catechesis of Erik is an example of what Stanley Hauerwas calls a "truthful community" or "community of character," a community capable of hearing the story of God and willing to live faithfully by it. Catechesis is immersion in the narrative that shapes the life of the church. The story of Israel, the story of Jesus, and the story of the church become Erik's story.

What is instructive here is the passion of those involved. Our church needs to see itself in the role of Erik's mother, as a relentless advocate for the faith formation of its people. I think of the pastor in Jersey City who walked the streets of his neighborhood before the opening of his confirmation classes to visit families. When one child did not show up for liturgy and Sunday school, he went to the housing project where the child lived and walked into the middle of a dope deal. One of the men whirled, pistol in hand, ready to shoot, then saw the pastor's collar and blurted out, "Jesus Christ, Father, I almost killed you!" The pastor nodded, walked up the stairs, and completed the call. We need to believe that the upbuilding of the faith of the people is a task worthy of giving our lives.

When pastors from our synod gathered with our national leaders after the September 11 tragedy, I told them that we had been ordained and baptized for this moment. I meant the immediate ministry of comfort and renewal as we attended to this tragedy among us. But I also meant the continuing work of our great high priest, helping to provide meaning to this altered world from the depths of our faith and the biblical drama. It is a priestly ministry of liturgy, articulation, peacemaking, programs of comfort and renewal, justice-seeking—and a ministry of Word and sacraments that embraces other faith journeys and a world hungry for a communal story.

Parking Lot Psalms

STEPHEN PAUL BOUMAN

Hebrews 5:1–10

So also Christ did not glorify himself in becoming a high priest, but was appointed by the one who said to him,
"You are my Son,
 today I have begotten you." (Hebrews 5:5)

"We are now seen by the world as having joined the ranks of those who know 'poverty' in a way we have not experienced it ever before. There have been wars, depressions, and tragedies of major proportions; but this one [September 11] somehow is different. This time the blow has staggered us…We are a people of great wealth and resources who for a moment have the opportunity to join Lazarus in a beggar's view of the world. We can learn an incredible lesson from down here about values and priorities, about needs and wants, about the way much of the rest of the world views us. It is an opportunity the rich man of the parable did not have until it was too late. It is the 'wisdom of the poor.' If we can grasp this wisdom, perhaps we will alter our prayer from 'God bless America' to 'God make America a blessing to all the nations of the world'" (Pastor Richard Michel, Trinity Lutheran Church, Staten Island).

The early believers grasped onto an image of Jesus as the priest who is in solidarity with humanity at its most vulnerable. The book of Hebrews gives us a vision of divine solidarity, "able to deal gently with the ignorant and wayward, since he himself is subject to weakness" (5:2). The one who "offered up prayers and supplications, with loud cries and tears" (5:7a), is the one who "learned obedience through what he suffered" (5:8b).

Ministries to and with the poor are usually the road not taken by seminaries, candidates, programs, initiatives, resources. The massive effort by the whole world to be at Ground Zero in person, prayer, and support magnifies the ground zeros we have missed: AIDS, spending more for jails than schools in some of our communities, the 20 million American children who go to bed hungry every night, the grinding poverty of much of the world. Jimmy Carter told us once that the hardest thing to do in this world is for a person in poverty and a person of privilege to be placed in the same room together.

Electra was four years old and lived with her mother in a welfare motel among prostitutes and drug abusers and the poorest of the poor. At a Thanksgiving dinner for the homeless, a pastor met Electra and her mother and invited them to stay with her for a weekend. Electra noticed that her new friends prayed before meals and implored them, "Please, teach me the God words." She then taught them to her neighbors in the motel. Her mother told us that the child could no longer bite into a peanut butter sandwich without making everyone around her say the God words.

Our great high priest chooses to stand with these people, and from their midst to renew the church and teach it once again the God words.

"Every high priest chosen from among mortals is put in charge of things pertaining to God on their behalf" (5:1).

When you invite the poor, they come. Edgar lived alone in the same motel as Electra. He often walked two miles to our church. He was a bit rough around the edges and would sometimes get loud and demanding. My heart sank on Palm Sunday when he was waiting in the sanctuary for me after a full day of liturgies, first communions, and pastoral conversations. I knew that Edgar would need a ride and some of my time, some bits and pieces of what I could produce toward his survival, and I wanted to go home.

On the drive back to his motel he talked my ear off and criticized the sermon. I prayed for patience. When I pulled into the parking lot of the run-down motor inn, a door opened and an elderly woman emerged. She knocked on another door, and another elderly woman peeked out. They limped to our car. Others waiting at the edges of the parking lot followed. I realized that they were expecting us. For the first time I noticed that Edgar's hand grasped a bunch of palms. He had promised to bring his neighbors palms from our liturgy.

With all his rough edges, Edgar was the only person who passed for a pastor in that backwater parish of broken souls. There could be no more fertile soil for biblical "church growth" than this concrete parking lot and these waiting children of God and their wisdom "from below."

He gave the elderly lady a palm branch through his window and she clutched her piece of palm as if it were the Hope diamond. I watched in awe as the palms from our liturgy were distributed among those like Jesus "in the days of his flesh" (5:7a). Edgar got out of the car. "Bless us!" he commanded me. I got out of the car, blessed their palms, placed my hands on each forehead, and pronounced benediction. If I had had bread and wine, I would have fed them right there.

"He is able to deal gently with the ignorant and wayward, since he himself is subject to weakness…So also Christ did not glorify himself in becoming a high priest, but was appointed by the one who said to him, 'You are my Son, / today I have begotten you'" (5:2, 5).

Our context for mission must have something to do with turning our church's life toward a motel of "priests forever, according to the order of Melchizedek" (5:6b), as well as the deep corporal and spiritual needs shared by all humanity in the solidarity at Ground Zero or Thailand after the tsunami or Baghdad. God willing, our lamentations are not the isolation and depression of wounded entitlement or private grief, but the community at the foot of the cross moving outward in solidarity and love toward the sorrow of the world for which Jesus "learned obedience through what he suffered" (5:8b).

Blind Spots

MARY W. ANDERSON

Mark 10:46–52

Then Jesus said to him, "What do you want me to do for you?" The blind man said to him, "My teacher, let me see again." (Mark 10:51)

Even the common lectionary cannot hold ecumenical friends together this Sunday. Some of us will depart from the scripture texts and focus on the Protestant Reformation of the sixteenth century. Some of us will center on the Mark 10 story of Jesus' encounter with Bartimaeus. I want to acknowledge these different directions and also reflect on the thematic connection between Bartimaeus's blindness and our history of reformation.

Healing stories in the gospels never seem to be simply a reversal of physical misfortune. A paralyzed man stands and walks. A man stretches out a withered hand to Jesus and sees it become useful again. A girl who was pronounced dead awakens. Particularly suspicious are the stories of those who "once were blind, but now they see." The connections between seeing and believing are so strong in the gospel accounts that these miracles worked through Jesus almost always seem more about growing in faith than taking off dark glasses. Though Bartimaeus was blind to many things, he clearly saw who Jesus was. Seeing "who Jesus is" is the goal of faith, and it leads to discipleship. Only the "unblind" can see where to follow. Indeed, at the end of the story we're told that this is exactly what happened. Bartimaeus regained his sight and followed Jesus on the way. Given that the very next verse in Mark narrates the entry into Jerusalem, the way Bartimaeus followed was the way to the cross.

Physical sight is not required for discipleship, but restoration is. Again and again in history, prophecy, and gospel, God works through miracle, through political forces, through social action, and through ordinary living to pick us up from where we have fallen and redirect us along right pathways. Blind Bartimaeus calls from the gutter until the Lord hears him. Then he returns to the Lord and is restored. I picture him, the last recruit in the discipleship army, marching toward Jerusalem with palm branch in hand.

Those who return to the Lord are restored, the Bible instructs. But how do we come to the point of return? Sometimes we make it sound easy and quick. I'm fairly skeptical of the 180 degree, born-again, overnight kind of return. Some changes are no doubt fast and immediate, but the changes that endure unto the generations are the result of a process of human or divine origin. Our returning to the Lord for restoration is a process that may be described in many ways.

Reformation is one of those ways. As people of the twenty-first century, we may be more in tune with some of reformation's synonyms, which also begin with "r": renovation, reorganization, restructuring. These are, interestingly, words we use in large corporate settings rather than small personal ones. The church, the corporate body of Christ, is a voice that calls for the wandering to return and then hosts the restoration banquet. To fulfill this mission, it must constantly be reforming. And yet most church folk know all too well that many "r" words can be fighting words in congregations. While many Protestant congregations (especially Lutheran ones) are willing to celebrate the Reformation of October 31, 1517, with pride and pomp, reformation's synonyms—renovate, reorganize, restructure—can be sources of conflict. All of these words indicate that something will be changed. And change is often heard as a synonym for "loss."

We enjoy 20/20 hindsight vision, proud of reformations past even as we are blind to the present need for reformation and restoration. This is true not only of the sixteenth century, but of the twentieth century as well. Our nation recently recognized the fortieth anniversary of Martin Luther King Jr.'s "I Have a Dream" speech. Though the reformation of racism in America is ongoing, much has changed in the past forty years. When King was preaching and protesting in the '60s, many of the adults in my life were shaking their southern heads and lamenting all the trouble he was causing. Decades later, this "troublemaker" is a martyr and a hero, whose birthday is a national holiday. I continue to be amazed at our collective blindness to the effects of racism and poverty in those days. My children shake their heads at the stories of segregation in schools, restaurants, and doctors' offices, unable to believe such things took place in their parents' lifetimes.

These are the rhythms of reformation. The troublemakers become heroes. The radical new ways eventually become beloved traditions. We are always moving from blindness to sightedness, from unfaithfulness to faithfulness. On days such as this, I am less interested in how the church was reformed than I am in recalling the lessons of reformation. Reformations teach us that we continue to need reform.

What corners of the church, of society, need serious reformation in this twenty-first century? Where are our blind spots? Will a reformer arise among us? Should one arise, what will we do to him or her? What do we allow to go unchallenged today that will one day cause our grandchildren to shake their heads at how blind we were to the gospel?

We disciples of Jesus have vision problems. We sometimes describe our blindness as an inability to see the forest for the trees, but that's a benign analysis. More worrisome is the inherited blindness of each generation, which so often assumes it is the best generation of all, with no lessons left to learn, only an inheritance to enjoy. This arrogance is the root of our blindness. We still need the miracle of restored sight.

Saints and Sinners

MARY W. ANDERSON

Mark 12:28–34

When Jesus saw that he answered wisely, he said to him, "You are not far from the kingdom of God." After that no one dared to ask him any question. (Mark 12:34)

It always breaks my heart a little when an elderly member of my congregation dies after decades of service and faithfulness. It breaks my heart a little more when only a handful of members attend the funeral of a shut-in. But on the Day of All Saints the names of these people who have passed on are read with reverence and thanks in front of the entire congregation. "For all the saints who from their labors rest," we sing.

Who are all these saints? Most churches don't generate much excitement by talking about the early saints (the ones with "St." in front of their names). Even though many of the hymns for this day refer to the saints of old who shone in glory, most of us prefer saints closer to home. Our communion of saints is a more familiar crowd—those who died in our congregations in the past year, our own parents and grandparents. We're also more apt to remember those famous saints who lived closer to our own lifetimes. Because we share the same century with them, we remember Mother Teresa and Cardinal Joseph Bernardin more often than St. Teresa or St. Joseph. It's a great day to remember all of those who have gone before us, the ones on whose shoulders we stand, the ones whose lives and witness have brought us to this new day.

We can study the history of our faith and proudly say we are where we are today because our ancestors in the faith raised their voices, made bold decisions, and prayed and taught the faith. We are where we are today because our ancestors were willing to go to jail, to be thrown to the lions, and be burned at the stake. We are here today because our ancestors fought for religious freedom, braved and explored a new world to establish churches in America, and spread the gospel. They did all these things because they loved Jesus, but also because they loved us, their descendants whom they would never know. They loved us so much that they wanted to make sure the story of the gospel was here for us. We are who we are today because of their faith, devotion, and bravery. Rise up, O saints of God!

But wait a minute. These saints were not our only ancestors. Isn't it also true that we are here today, that we are who we are, in the condition in which we find ourselves, because we also had biological and spiritual ancestors who sat on their hands, who cared only for themselves, who thought little about the impact of their actions on future generations? We are also the products of those who were apathetic in their witness. We are the biological and spiritual descendants, for example, of those who advocated a racially segregated society. We are related to people who argued against women's ordination. And we may have to admit that some in our heritage shrugged their shoulders in the face of oppression and greed. We are products both of those ancestors who fought for the faith and of those who fought against the faith. We are the descendants of both sets of grandparents. We have saints in our blood and skeletons in our closets.

Congregations, too, are the spiritual grandchildren of wonderful stewards who gave their all, and of generations of curmudgeons who threw water on the Spirit's fire every chance they got. What type of ancestor do we, who by baptism are part of the communion of saints, hope to be?

One of these All Saints Days our names will be read. We are the potential saints for future generations. We are the shoulders on which others will stand. Will we be ancestors who sat on their hands or ancestors who raised their hands? Sometimes we forget that we aren't just living our busy lives. We're also laying a foundation, molding a future, and establishing a legacy. How is it going?

"There breaks a yet more glorious day / saints triumphant rise in bright array. Will we leave a legacy of justice, or will we leave a bequest of selfishness? Those we admire as witnesses to Christ are the ones we believe are our best examples of living the simple commands of Jesus to love God with our whole selves, and our neighbor as ourselves. Those who do, Jesus said, are not far from the kingdom of God. Being a saint means living in hope and not in despair. It means forgiving, not judging; loving, not despising; lifting up, not tearing down. Being a saint means that you can mock evil (what we do on Halloween) rather than being afraid of it or controlled by it.

In this dying of the year, this time of harvest, we would do well to take stock as well as reminisce. When the low G sounds on the organ, announcing the beginning of R. Vaughan Williams's tune to the hymn "For All the Saints," I feel as though the rumbling of that low bass note calls us to worship the communion of saints. It is a call to St. Peter and St. Paul, to Mary Magdalene and Mother Teresa, to Martin Luther and Martin Luther King Jr. As we remember these strong shoulders on which we stand, we are challenged to strengthen our own shoulders. We are ancestors in the making, after all, of saints for a generation yet unborn. It is an awesome opportunity. Rise up, O saints of God!

Widow's Walk

MARY W. ANDERSON

Mark 12:38–44

> *Then he called his disciples and said to them, "Truly I tell you, this poor widow has put in more than all those who are contributing to the treasury." (Mark 12:43)*

Jesus has warned before that the rich will have it hard at the entrance to the kingdom. Now he praises the poor widow's offering and makes it clear that the standard measurement for assessing gifts is not how much we give to the work of God or how much we put in the offering plate, but how much we have left for ourselves. Those who give out of their abundance still have abundance left. And that's a problem.

Can it really be that the poor are praised, that this widow is lifted up, because she gave every bit of money in her bank account? Is this what it takes to follow Jesus? Why this preference for poverty in Jesus' teaching?

Does it sometimes seem that Jesus is romanticizing and idealizing the poor? Surely the poor would be the first to object. Life in poverty is what we all want to avoid, not aspire to. No one dreams of growing up poor, of living from government check to government check, of digging through garbage cans, or living in run-down apartments with no heat.

The woman at the temple was not a poor widow; she was poor because she was a widow. My understanding of sociology and economics in first-century Palestine tells me there was no such thing as a rich widow in that culture. Women were totally dependent on their male relatives for their livelihood. To be widowed meant not only losing someone you may have loved; but, more tragically, it also meant that you were losing the one on whom you were totally dependent. Widows were forced to live off of the good graces of other male relatives and anyone in the community who might provide a meal here, a little money there.

The two little coins in the woman's hand were probably all she had. The truth is—and the extremely poor know this well—those coins weren't going to change her life. When you've got so little, a penny or two isn't going to move you from welfare to work. She could be at peace and joyful in knowing she was able to give to the temple treasury, because with the coins or without them, she was still a dependent person.

Rich people, like most of us readers, can't say the same. My money gives me independence and freedom from living like a poor widow. I like it that way and my family likes it that way, so I will not be putting my entire paycheck in the offering plate on Sunday. But I've also seen poor homeless people in worship who are anxious to find an offering envelope so they can give the only dollar in their pocket toward God's work. When you're that low on the economic scale, giving isn't the problem; getting is.

The widow wasn't dependent on her money or her status in life; she had none of these. She was dependent on God and her neighbor for everything. She didn't have two feet to stand on; she didn't have bootstraps to pull up. She was totally dependent—and that's what Jesus pulls out of her story like a pearl of great price. This is what we are to be like before God—dependent on nothing but the grace of God. We are to be people without any resources except the riches of God's mercy.

The issue is not how much we have in the bank, but what that money is for us. Is it our heart, our security, our source of power, or is it a tool for our stewardship? Are we dependent on our money to give us all we want and need from life, or are we dependent on God to make us rich? If you follow me, Jesus teaches, you will walk in the way of the widow. Live lives that show in everything you do and say that you are dependent on God for all you have and all you are.

As good Americans we've been taught to celebrate our independence, but Jesus teaches us to celebrate our great dependence on God alone. If independence is a sign of strength and success, how can we possibly rejoice in dependence?

Our culture counsels us to become like the honored scribes, but Jesus counsels us to become like the dishonored widow. We are to model our lives on one we would normally overlook, being too busy admiring the lifestyles of the rich and famous.

The widow tossed the only shred of independence she had into the offering plate, but she kept intact her complete dependence on God and neighbor. She is our spiritual mentor standing there on the margins of all we hold dear. Her way is a life of faith grounded in the love of God, the grace of our Lord Jesus Christ, and the communion of the Holy Spirit. It's a life lived in the conviction that we are stewards of all we have in our hands and our lives, not the owners of these things.

Where previously we connected dependence with oppression and depression, Jesus shows us that our dependence on God leads to joy and thanksgiving. If God is running the universe and ruling my life, I no longer have to save myself, prove myself, or justify myself. I'm the work of God's hands. I rest and work in those hands, and I shall die in those hands. To be free of those hands would be death to me, because in them is life abundant.

We give thanks for the widow's great witness. May we be as free as she is.

Time's Up

MARY W. ANDERSON

Mark 13:1–8

"When you hear of wars and rumors of wars, do not be alarmed; this must take place, but the end is still to come." (Mark 13:7)

As the leaves fall from the trees and the earth goes brown and bare, the church contemplates the end as well—the end of our lives in death and the end of the world with Christ's coming. The very idea that there will be an end is threatening to those of us who have pretty good lives and good plans for the future. For those of us who experience life as a roller coaster of ups and downs, on the other hand, or those who experience life as mostly downs, the idea of "an end to it all" may be comforting.

Those among us who are very elderly or very ill think often about the end of our lives. We prepare and put things in order. Those of us who aren't ill or elderly are busy living in the middle of things. But what if we all needed to prepare for the end?

What if you knew you had only one month left in your life?

- Would you finish up important matters at work?
- Would you travel to a place you always wanted to go?
- Would you pray more, go to church more, do that generous act you always wanted to do for others?
- Would you find ways to leave a mark on the world?
- Would you reconcile a fractured friendship?

By answering yes to one or more of these possibilities, we indicate that in our last days we would be better stewards of all the things God has given us in this life—better than we are now. In the intensity of last days, we would live better, be better. We would be more generous, more focused on the most important things in life. The question is: Why do we need to be under threat of death to be better stewards?

Here's another "what if." What if we discovered that our congregation only had one more month to exist? If my congregation only had a month to live, I would want all the members to be together as much as possible. If only for one precious Sunday, I'd like to have everybody listed in our church directory together for worship. If our time as a congregation was almost over, I don't think we'd have much trouble getting inactive or barely active members and friends to join us. End times have that kind of power.

As members of a congregation at the end of its life, we would also have the great opportunity to decide what we wanted to do with our assets. Provided God or the bishop left that up to us, we would have a few million dollars worth of real estate, cash, and furnishings to disperse back into the local community and the Christian community.

How would we decide what to do with the money? We wouldn't have time to fight about it. We'd have to focus fast and get our priorities straight. What would we support, and what would we want our final legacy to be? We could help start a new ministry where none currently exists. Or we could support an existing one, endow scholarships, build a youth center in town, or a better shelter for the homeless. We could do so much—if we had only a month left! We could be really great stewards of our resources—if we only had a month to live.

The question is, why is it so hard for our congregations to consider this kind of stewardship if we have another hundred years to live? The Bible's teaching about the end times reminds us that we have failed to see history from God's perspective. There is a bigger picture than just the snapshot of our lives. We don't live in the moment; we live in all of history.

Yes, there's an impracticality to living as if it were the end when it's really not. If I knew my life would really be over in a month, I probably would jump on a plane and visit some places I've longed to see. But if I've got much more than a month, I have bills to pay and obligations to tend. Living as if it's the end would be irresponsible. But does our best stewardship have to exist only in our imaginings of "what ifs"?

Jesus calls us to do both: to live with the intensity of last days while living our regular lives. He reminds us that we are not ultimately invested in this world, and he liberates us to work with courage, with hope. End times call for tall towers of hope. They call for a lightning-speed reordering of priorities. End times call for alertness, sharpness. They tingle with expectation. They are times of uncertainty and fear only for those whose faith is thin.

While the end of the world could be millennia away for all we know, and while we expect our congregations to continue their ministries well into this new century, end times are around us. Church historians and culture-watchers tell us that we're on the edge of an end time for the church's traditional role in society. But this doesn't mean things are over. As Jesus said, you will hear of wars and earthquakes and famines, but it doesn't mean the end is near. You will hear of the comings and goings of institutions and cultures, but it doesn't mean the end is near. It may only be, Jesus says, the beginning of what God has planned. End times are powerful times pregnant with purpose for those with ears to hear and eyes to see the advent of our God.

Royal Treatment

Mary W. Anderson

John 18:33–37

Then Pilate entered the headquarters again, summoned Jesus, and asked him, "Are you the King of the Jews?" (John 18:33)

Another church year ends on November 23 with the festival of Christ the King. Although a few folks get jazzed over this festival, most of us need to be reminded that the church year is different from the calendar year, the academic year, and the budget year.

On most minor and major church festivals, I remind my congregation how ancient these festivals are. I like to wow them with the vast number of centuries the church has been observing some of them. The festival of Christ the King spoils that plan. It was first introduced in 1925, and not until 1969 was it designated the festival for the last Sunday of the church year. Since I cannot wow them with a millennium's worth of tradition, I emphasize how the church continues to create traditions and make liturgical history.

It is odd to think that the twentieth-century church developed a festival centering on Christ's image as king. In America we are as distanced from the image of "king" as we are from the image of "shepherd." Popular theology is more intrigued with the image of Jesus as CEO—a leadership role, to be sure, but hardly comparable to that of a king with a kingdom.

Our American brush with royalty comes mostly from Britain. We might not be able to name any kings, but we are familiar with Queen Elizabeth and with the tabloids and tragedies surrounding her family. We would easily recognize the queen, yet many of us are unaware of what she really does from day to day and what her powers really are. Royalty is respected; it's part of the tradition; but does it really do anything? Do we need it?

I wonder and worry that people perceive Christ's rule to be similar to the queen of England's rule. Do we view Christ as one surrounded with the art and beauty of a tradition that is more antique than active? Do we see this figure of salvation as hopelessly outdated and practically mute in these postmodern times?

If we stretch ourselves to think in royal terms, we remember that although "king" may be an unfamiliar symbol, it is a political term. Kings rule a particular piece of geography. They may rule over a particular ethnic group. They have subjects—they have "a people." What we declare on this last Sunday of the church year is: Christ has made of us a people.

Growing up in the South, I often heard the home folks ask of a son's girlfriend, "Who are her people?" They were fishing for two things: a family name and a location. "She's one of the Wingards from over Lexington way." This information could make one be embraced or shunned. I never heard "people" used outside of family until I moved out of the overwhelmingly Christian South and lived in Chicago. Here, "my people" was used for distinct ethnic groups and religious groups. And it was an unspoken truth that if any significant rubber ever hit any significant road, it was your people that mattered. A "people" was not a biological unit. They didn't necessarily share DNA but perhaps things more bonding: a common story, the foods and meals they ate together, the experiences they endured, and the hopes that endure through generations. I envied their sense of solidarity and identity. It's good to have a people.

Those who have been baptized into Christ Jesus are the people of his pasture and the sheep of his hand. Christ has made of us a people with his kingship. And that kingship is unique, unlike any earthly kingship that is bound by geographic borders. This kingdom is boundless. Christ's rule is not limited to a particular racial or national group. All are welcome, especially the chronically unwelcome ones. Christ reigns from the cross, we say. Christ rules, as many earthly rulers do, because he has waged battle and has been victorious. But Christ's enemies are sin, death, and the devil, all defeated by Christ's death. In a kingdom of a lowly stable and an empty tomb, death birthed life.

To speak of kings and kingdoms, of subjects and peoples, requires a fair amount of translation for modern ears. Some, finding the translation too cumbersome, will opt for calling Jesus their CEO or therapist. But what will then be truly lost is not the title used, but the relationship implied.

To say Christ is king implies that we are subjects. The heart of this relationship is our dependence on a ruler who holds our lives in his hands. We do not choose a ruler as we elect a president, hire a CEO, or contract with a therapist. We are Christ's people—we share the same eucharistic foods, we share the same story of faith, we stake our lives on the same hopes.

Here at the end of the church year, after living through another cycle of hearing the story of Jesus' life, of being taught by him in miracle and parable, we come to the coda of this hymn of praise. After another year of living our lives, burying our dead, baptizing our babies, marrying and divorcing, struggling and thriving, we bring all of the year's experiences to the climax of this day. We lay it all back at the feet of the one enthroned on the cross, giving thanks. It's great to be a people ruled in love and mercy.